Fear and Conventionality

To

ALL WHO SAY:

"HUMAN NATURE IS THE SAME THE WORLD OVER"

Fear and Conventionality

By

Elsie Clews Parsons, Ph.D.

Author of
"The Family," "The Old-Fashioned Woman," etc.

With a New Introduction by
Desley Deacon

The University of Chicago Press
Chicago and London

The University of Chicago Press, Chicago 60637
The University of Chicago Press, Ltd., London

Introduction © 1997 by
The University of Chicago
Originally published 1914 by
G. P. Putnam's Sons, New York and London.
University of Chicago Press Edition 1997
Printed in the United States of America
03 02 01 00 99 98 97   6 5 4 3 2 1

Library of Congress Cataloging-in-Publication Data

Parsons, Elsie Worthington Clews, 1874–1941.
   Fear and conventionality / by Elsie Clews Parsons ;
with a new introduction by Desley Deacon.
      p.   cm.
   Originally published: New York : Putnam's, 1914.
   Includes bibliographical references and index.
   ISBN 0-226-64746-3 (alk. paper)
      1. Manners and customs.   2. Ethnology—United
States.   3. Middle class—United States.
   4. Interpersonal relations—United States.   5. United
States—Social life and customs.   I. Title.
GT75.P3   1997
390—dc21   97-1996
                                                      CIP

The paper used in this publication meets the minimum
   requirements of the American National Standard for
   Information Sciences—Permanence of Paper for Printed
   Library Materials, ANSI Z39.48–1984.

INTRODUCTION

DESLEY DEACON

TO Randolph Bourne, that connoisseur of all things new and modern, feminist anthropologist and sociologist Elsie Clews Parsons exemplified the Modern Mind. "In an American intellectual world still too much divided between hopelessly unporous science and popular sentimentality," he wrote in 1917, "her mind is a fortunate anomaly"—and, he added, "there is none more compelling."[1]

Parsons was compelling for Bourne because she was, like him, a practical modernist, concerned above all with how people live. As Bourne put it, she always engaged "the raw material of living." She combined this engagement with a clear vision of how people could live; and she presented this combination in a distinctively

Desley Deacon is the author of *Elsie Clews Parsons: Inventing Modern Life* (1997). She is also the author of *Managing Gender: The State, the New Middle Class and Women Workers 1830–1930* (1989) and coauthor of *Elites in Australia* (1979).

spare and ironic style that amused and startled without losing either human sympathy or scientific authority. Always ethnologist, educator, and prophet (or, we could say, artist), she wanted her science to educate people about the possibilities open to them, and to inspire them to become "inventors of the future."

Fear and Conventionality, published in November 1914, demonstrates most clearly the combination of entertainment, shock, education, and invention that was Elsie Clews Parsons's trademark during the years 1912 to 1916. Written in that golden period immediately before World War I, it captures a modernist spirit of youth and optimism that gives way in her *Social Freedom* (1915) and *Social Rule* (1916) to more somber reflections on the intractability of racial and tribal loyalties and divisions. At the same time, *Fear and Conventionality* conveys Parsons's new self-assurance in her role as professional ethnologist and public intellectual that culminated in 1941 with her election as the first female president of the American Anthropological Association.[2]

Fear and Conventionality represented a major transition in Parsons's life and work. In 1914 she was forty years old. The daughter of a wealthy

New York banker and his socialite wife, she avoided with great determination the society life into which she was born—studying the new science of sociology under Franklin Giddings at Barnard, working in the burgeoning settlement movement, and gaining a Ph.D. from Columbia in 1899. Over the next twelve years, she combined an "experimental" marriage to Republican politician Herbert Parsons and the birth of six children with a career, first as fieldwork director and teacher of sociology at Barnard and Columbia, then, after Herbert was elected to Congress, as a commentator on current sexual and family arrangements.[3]

The Washington years—from 1905 to 1911—were difficult, marked by continual pregnancies, the tragedy of losing two babies at birth, obsessive jealousy over Herbert's admiration for a conventional woman friend, and anxiety that her controversial opinions might damage Herbert's career. A trip to the Southwest in 1910 stimulated Elsie's interest in Pueblo culture; and Herbert's electoral defeat and their return to New York the following year allowed her to develop an important new relationship with a group of young anthropologists—all students or allies of Columbia professor Franz Boas—with whom she felt an immediate intellectual sympathy. At the same time, she became involved in the new feminist movement, joining the New York group, Heterodoxy, which emphasized diversity and "the creation of a new consciousness in women." Strengthened by these new friendships, Parsons painfully remade her family life during 1913 and 1914 on the basis of a set of "modern" principles she advocated in public and lived by in private for the rest of her life. Rather more exuberantly, she also began in 1913 to articulate her vision of what social science should be and do. *Fear and Conventionality* is, therefore, the culmination of Parsons's early preoccupations, personal and intellectual, and a harbinger of many of the directions her work took as she became centrally involved in the world of Boasian anthropology.[4]

Fear and Conventionality is above all a devastating critique of the native-born, middle-class American family, based on her careful observations of her own social milieu and a breathtaking range of reading about other cultures. Placing the American family indiscriminately beside the Fijian or the Ugandan, Parsons scrutinizes the conventionalities of family life—the taken-for-granted ways in which relationships within and surrounding this most intimate of worlds are institutionalized and stripped of any personal quality. People are afraid of strangers and require great inducements to travel beyond home, she argues; and the elaborate etiquette surrounding entertaining, introductions, and making new acquaintances serves to "disinfect" the home against contamination by outsiders. Within this conservative haven, strict separation by sex and age is enforced. "As the closest of relations between unlike persons and therefore the most to be apprehended," marriage and the relations between parents and children are, she concludes, the most hedged in by minor, but exacting, ceremonial.[5]

Parsons's interest in the ethnography of family life began in childhood as she observed her parents' empty marriage and struggled against her family's constricting gender expectations. She saw her own marriage as an experiment (at least for her own class and race) in developing new family relationships, and in combining marriage, work, and childbearing. Her experience of teaching through her first two pregnancies in 1901 and 1903 pushed her beyond the studies of working-class and immigrant families she supervised as director of sociological fieldwork and in the settlement movement. Convinced that women like herself needed to "get an ethnological inkling of themselves" before they presumed to understand—let alone critique—those of other classes and cultures, she began to systematically observe her own social set. In 1905, Parsons began her long career as a public intellectual with a series of challenging articles and a textbook on the family for college students and home reading groups, published in 1906. Treating the American family as but one of many ways in which sex and reproduction are organized, *The Family* ends with a vision of a new "democratic" and open set of arrangements that include the valuation of sexual passion—especially for women—trial marriage, divorce, contraception, and "productive" wives and mothers.[6]

The scandal caused by Parsons's advocacy of these ideas, coming on top of her reproductive tragedies and Herbert's election to Congress, silenced her publicly until she returned to New York and to health at the end of 1911. But during her early New York years she had established both her basic methodology and her moral stance. Parsons's greatest influence was the French sociologist Gabriel Tarde, whose

Laws of Imitation she translated as an under-
graduate. From Tarde's wide-ranging work she
selected elements that guided her throughout
her career: the idea of social science as an aid
to invention rather than an instrument of social
control; a suspicion of all-encompassing theories
(what we would now call "metanarratives"); an
interest in the psychological factors that influence cultural choices; an emphasis on the cre-
ative individual as the catalyst for social change;
and the importance of what Tarde called "conversation" or "the logical duel" in thrashing out
rival ideas and promoting cultural and social
tolerance, flexibility, and inventiveness.[7]

Tarde's influence was immediately evident
when Elsie Clews (not yet married) began to
study tenement house families in 1899. Aban-
doning the economic focus of Le Play's standard
family monograph method, she decided that
"the real life of the tenements" was revealed by
the "neglected psychological social fact." As a
reviewer observed of Parsons's innovative "Barnard method," she and her students studied the
social group as if it were a tribe, characterized
above all by beliefs and superstitious customs,
and they attempted to reproduce family life "in
all its complexity and detail." When Parsons be-

gan to note down the mores of her own social set
in 1904, it was their beliefs and superstitions,
and the little ceremonials that sustained these,
that interested her most. In 1913, she saw this
focus on the present-day psychological function
of ceremonial as one of the most important contributions she could make to Boasian anthropology. As she put it in the *American Anthropologist*
in 1915, referring dryly to anthropologists' pen-
chant for "salvage ethnology," "A dying out
type of psychosis [in a living culture] may be in
even more urgent need of description than a dying out people."[8]

Tarde's influence was also decisive in Parsons's resolve to take on the role of public pro-
moter of controversial "conversation." Always
committed to living out her convictions, she also
decided, sometime around 1905, that she had a
responsibility as a privileged woman to speak
out on issues where others might be more severely penalized; and, although she was a very
private person, she gave personal testimony
throughout her life on issues such as birth control, because, she felt, this was "more telling
than any other argument."[9]

Parsons was committed, therefore, to a psy-
chologically-oriented ethnography of everyday

foot-binding in China. Parsons felt that even the
new anthropology tacitly pandered to misinfor-
mation about such issues by its concentration
on nonliterate societies. Laying out her intellectual approach to Franz Boas in 1913, she argued
that the distinction between "ethnologies" of
"primitive" and "histories" of "civilized" cultures was artificial, "and a remarkable, if unre-
marked, instance of folklore." In her opinion,
observations of "civilized" and "primitive"
peoples were equally important to ethnology;
and studies of cultural elements required comparative data from so-called civilized and primitive alike. Indeed, she pointed out, such
comparative studies were likely to find a mixture of the "civilized" and the "primitive" in
both types of society. In a series of articles on
ceremonial, Parsons urged her new colleagues to
pay more attention to the psychological factors
involved in such standard anthropological preoccupations as avoidance and teknonymy; they
would gain greater insight into these phenomena, she argued, if they first recognized them in
their own society. Finally, in private letters,
newspaper articles, and an elaborate plan for a
school of ethnology that never came to fruition,
she insisted that anthropology was such an im-

portant educational tool that its practitioners had a duty to make their work accessible to the general public.[11]

Fear and Conventionality is Parsons's most important early attempt to put these principles into practice. Its observations of current sexual and family mores are based on two unpublished but carefully-crafted ethnographies/memoirs/diaries, "The Imaginary Mistress" (1913) and "The Journal of a Feminist, 1913–1914," in which Parsons systematically reports on New York upper-class and intellectual culture as a native informant might to a visiting ethnographer. Parsons has also scoured etiquette books—with which her feminist friends gleefully supplied her—and memoirs to build up the picture of "civilized" ceremonial she places side-by-side with that of so-called savage society.[12]

But Parsons's intended audience is not only—or even primarily—other anthropologists and sociologists. The new cultural anthropology to which Parsons had allied herself was part of a larger intellectual movement to recreate knowledge, art, and personal life that was becoming known as modernism. Nurtured by philosophers of science such as Ernst Mach, philosophers such as William James and Henri Bergson, nov-

elists such as H. G. Wells, and sexologists such
as Havelock Ellis, modernism burst onto popular consciousness between 1909 and 1913. As one
of Tarde's "inventors of the future," Parsons
had been an early pioneer of a practical modernism concerned with refashioning personal life.
In close-knit intellectual and artistic communities such as New York's Greenwich Village, she
now found an audience eager, in equal parts, to
be instructed, amused, and inspired.

It was for this audience of young modernists
that Parsons developed the eclectic mixture of
modernism, feminism, and anthropology represented in *Fear and Conventionality*. In *The Old-
Fashioned Woman: Primitive Fancies about the Sex*,
published the previous year, she had experimented with a dry, ironic, modernist style in
which she parodied "salvage ethnology," ex-
ploded the category of "primitive," indiscriminately mixed times and places, and swamped the
reader with "a lethal bath of facts" demonstra-
ting that the outmoded concept "woman" was
kept alive only by the bizarre rituals of the Elders. *Fear and Conventionality* and its successors
Social Freedom (1915) and *Social Rule* (1916) continue this distinctive style, which Parsons also
uses in the numerous articles she published in

the *Masses*, the *New Review*, the *New Republic*, and other popular intellectual magazines during this period. Each of these books focuses on a contemporary psychosis revealed by the rituals she describes: *Fear and Conventionality* on the fear of sincere interaction that maintains social distance and cripples relationships; *Social Freedom* on the urge to classify that constricts the development of personality; and *Social Rule* on the urge to control—in Nietzsche's term—the will to power, which maintains status and discourages innovation. These three books also present a picture of the world Parsons imagines freed by cross-cultural understanding from unnecessary and harmful ceremonial. In the final, highly distinctive, chapter of *Fear and Conventionality*, Parsons paints her most complete picture of this "Unconventional Society," where willingness to change is a virtue; difference is valued; caste exclusiveness is discouraged; and travel and new experience are sought after. In such a society, Parsons imagines an entirely different family life based on sincerity, privacy, and genuine passion.[13]

At the numerous discussion groups that sprang up during these years, such as the salon of her friend Mabel Dodge, Parsons's outra-

geous but thoughtful ideas provided grist for discussions of the new woman, the new family, and
the new community. Her readers enjoyed what
the *New Republic* called her "natural history of
the right thing." For *Masses* editor Floyd Dell,
it was "a delightful and dangerous book"—a
book on manners as an expression of the soul
that was equal only to Veblen in being both al-
luring and profound. The crusty iconoclast
H. L. Mencken considered it the only piece of
social science, apart from Nietzsche's work, that
was of any use, because it dealt with "that pow-
erful complex of assumptions, prejudices, instinctive reactions, racial emotions, and
unbreakable vices of mind which enters so mas-
sively into the daily thinking of all of us." Even
William Ogburn, that pioneer of statistical sociology, found her methodology "scientifically
convincing." "When dice are rolled many times
and the distribution of the results is noted," he
wrote in a review of *Social Rule*, "it can be told
whether the dice are loaded or whether they follow the laws of chance. Although the calculus of
probabilities for customs has not been worked
out, yet such an amassing of plausible illustration as is contained in this volume seems to es-

tablish a high degree of probability for the thesis."[14]

Parsons's anthropological colleagues were less sure of how to deal with her popular work. At a time when American Museum of Natural History president Henry Fairfield Osborn considered most anthropology little more than the gossip of natives, the new cultural anthropologists were battling for acceptance as detached "scientists." Yet they all recognized in Parsons's committed public stance the passion for social change that fueled their work. Although they teased her about being a "propagandist," a "moralist," and even a "psychologist," they eagerly read and discussed her books. As Alfred Kroeber, Parsons's close friend and sometime lover, wrote in 1922, "My congratulations on you'll be surprised what. I read again today the last chapter of Fear and Conventionality. I can't yet agree everywhere . . . but a something that underlies and shines through stirs me and wins me." Pliny Goddard, closer in temperament to Parsons, wrote of the "understanding thrill" he got from *Social Freedom:* "In time others will appreciate it too. In fact they do appreciate it, but one thinks it is cold science and another hope-

less propaganda. I know it is a poet's vision."
He also was more prescient about the potential
influence of her work. In the first volume of the
American Anthropologist under his editorship, he
acknowledged that *Fear and Conventionality* was
only incidentally the sort of book they usually
reviewed: "Anthropology poses as a pure science. . . . It is not concerned with values and
has no conscious desire to make practical appli-
cations. . . . In America, at least, it is inclined to
ignore all people who can read and write as too
sophisticated for its attention." He continued,

> It will surprise all of us and please some of us
> to observe with what effect the facts of ethnol-
> ogy can be used in the solution of present-day
> problems. These customs of past and passing
> peoples are not merely interesting and curious
> facts. Properly arranged, they teach the pop-
> ular readers for whom the book is written that
> the ways of the so-called barbarous peoples
> are not so very different from our own. The
> ethnological readers of the book, too, will be
> surprised to find that the customs of New
> York and Washington after all are not radi-
> cally different from those of Australia.

"Sometime in the future Dr Parsons's book may
be a source of ethnological information concerning the inhabitants of the United States of the

twentieth century," Goddard concluded. "She is by no means an indifferent observer."[15]

As Americans succumbed to nationalist and racist hysteria during the war that broke out just as *Fear and Conventionality* went to press, Parsons lost faith in the power of anthropology to make rapid changes in public opinion. Her work continued to be driven by a passion to open people's minds and revitalize their lives, but she turned, from 1917, to long-term studies of acculturation processes in Pueblo and New World African cultures. Although the audience and the focus were different, this work continued Parsons's interest in psychological factors in cultural choices made by people in on-going cultures. Her influence in anthropology was subtle but decisive: by the 1930s a new generation had placed psychology at the center of the discipline; acculturation studies threatened to take over the *American Anthropologist*; autobiographies by native informants were an established genre; and anthropologists experimented with ways to make their work accessible and useful to the public. When Margaret Mead published her pathbreaking *Coming of Age in Samoa* in 1928, Parsons wrote enthusiastically to Boas, "Margaret Mead is a more sophisticated young woman than most of us. She did not have to go to Samoa for an analysis of what is lacking in our culture, but her Samoan comparisons will give her greater authenticity as a best seller. For the last ten years, there has been a real craving in circles of the higher journalism for the very thing she has produced."[16]

She might have added that she had played an important part, with *Fear and Conventionality* and her other early works of "higher journalism," in creating that appetite.

---

1. Randolph Bourne, "A Modern Mind, Review of Elsie Clews Parsons, *Social Rule*," *Dial*, 22 March 1917, 239–40.

2. Elsie Clews Parsons, *Social Freedom: A Study of the Conflicts between Social Classifications and Personality* (New York: G. P. Putnam's Sons, 1915), and *Social Rule: A Study of the Will to Power* (New York: G. P. Putnam's Sons, 1916).

3. See Desley Deacon, *Elsie Clews Parsons: Inventing Modern Life* (Chicago: University of Chicago Press, 1997).

4. Marie Howe, "Feminism," *New Review*, August 1914, 441. For Parsons's feminist ethics, see "Marriage and Parenthood—a Distinction," *International Journal of Ethics*, July 1915, 514–17, "When Mating and Parenthood are Theoretically Distinguished," January 1916, 207–16, and "Feminism and Sex Ethics," July 1916, 462–65.

5. Parsons, *Fear and Conventionality* (New York: G. P. Putnam's Sons, 1914), 155.

6. Parsons, *The Family: An Ethnographical and Historical Outline, with Descriptive Notes, planned as a Text-book for the use of College Lecturers and Directors of Home-Reading Clubs* (New York: G. P. Putnam's Sons, 1906).

7. Parsons, trans., *The Laws of Imitation*, by Gabriel Tarde,

Introduction

with an introduction by Franklin H. Giddings (New York: Henry Holt and Company, 1903). Translated from *Les Lois de l'imitation,* 2d ed. (Paris, 1895) in 1896. For scandal, see *New York Times* [*NYT*], 18 November 1906, 1, and 19 November 1906, 5.

8. Elsie W. Clews, "Field Work in Teaching Sociology," *Educational Review* 19 (September 1900): 159–69; M. H. [M. Halbwachs], review of Elsa G. Herzfeld, *Family Monographs, L'Année sociologique* (1905–6): 605–8, esp. 605; Parsons, "Interpreting Ceremonialism," *American Anthropologist* [*AA*] 17 (July–September 1915): 600–603, esp. 603. See "The Le Play Method of Monographs on Families," trans. Charles A. Ellwood, *American Journal of Sociology* [*AJS*] (March 1897): 662–79.

9. Parsons, "Little Essays in Lifting Taboo," unpublished manuscript, 1906, 1–4, and Notes, misc. no. 2, [1908], Elsie Clews Parsons papers, American Philosophical Society Library [APS].

10. Robert H. Lowie, "Social Organization," *AJS* 20 (July 1914): 68–97, and "A New Conception of Totemism," *Journal of American Folklore* [*JAFL*] 24 (1911): 189–207. See Paul Radin, "Personal Reminiscences of a Winnebago Indian," *JAFL* 26 (1913): 293–318; and Pliny Goddard, "The Relation of Folk-Lore to Anthropology," *JAFL* 28 (1915): 18–23.

11. Parsons to Franz Boas, draft, [December 1913?], APS; Parsons, "Avoidance," and "Teknonymy," *AJS* 19 (January and March 1914): 480–84 and 649–50; Parsons to Robert H. Lowie, 6 February 1914, Lowie Papers, University of California, Berkeley; Parsons, "Ethnology in Education," *New Review,* April 1914, 228–29, "Home Study in Ethnology." *AA* 17 (April–June 1915): 409–11, "Making Ethnology Popular," *New York Tribune,* 30 January 1916, sec. 5, 1, and "The School of Ethnology [Social History]: A University Extension School" [1914?], Parsons Family papers, Rye Historical Society [RHS]. See biologist William T. Sedgwick: "Feminist Revolutionary Principle is Biological Bosh," *NYT,* 18 January 1914, sec. 5, 2; and missionary Helen Montgomery, *Western Women in Eastern Lands,* and *Handbook of Suggestions to Accompany the Text-book* (New York: Macmillan, 1910).

12. Parsons, "The Imaginary Mistress" (1913), and "The Journal of a Feminist, 1913–1914," unpublished manuscripts, APS.

13. *The Old-Fashioned Woman: Primitive Fancies about the Sex* (New York: G. P. Putnam's Sons, 1913).

14. "Fear and Conventionality," *New Republic*, 19 December 1914, 26–27; Floyd Dell, *New Review*, 1 January 1916, 17–18; H. L. Mencken, "The Genealogy of Etiquette," *Prejudices: First Series* (New York: Knopf, 1919), 150–70, esp. 156; William F. Ogburn, *Political Science Quarterly* 32 (Dec. 1917): 641–43. See also *NYT Book Review*, 27 December 1914, 587; *Boston Transcript*, 2 January 1915, 8; *Outlook*, 10 February 1915, 348; Victor E. Helleberg, *AJS* 22 (September 1916): 274–75; Signe Toksvig, "Elsie Clews Parsons," *New Republic*, 26 November 1919, 17–20.

15. Alfred L. Kroeber to Parsons, [April] 1922, RHS; Pliny Goddard to Parsons, 26 January 1916, APS; Pliny Goddard, *AA* 17 (April–June 1915): 343–44. See J. M. Kennedy, "Philanthropy and Science in New York City: The American Museum of Natural History, 1868–1968" (Ph.D. diss., Yale University, 1968), 163.

16. Parsons to Franz Boas, 23 October 1928, Franz Boas professional papers, APS.

CONTENTS

Contents

PREFACE

So wont are we by way of disclaimer to call a man in a fit of temper or lust a beast or a savage that likenesses of another kind between us and other creatures, essential likenesses, too, we overlook. Like other expressions of racial pride, this particular trick of castigation dulls our observation, and even leads us astray; for is it not in our reputed virtues rather than in our crying vices that we most resemble our so-called inferiors, beast or savage, in our orderly habits rather than in our lapses? Are not we all of us extremely conservative and usually far more staid than passionate? To all of us, to the animal, to the savage, and to the civilized being few experiences are as uncomfortable or painful, as disquieting or fearful, as the call to innovate. Adaptations we all of us dislike or hate. We dodge or shirk them as best we may. And we have protected ourselves against having to make them as well as we could. Our safeguards are variously known as "instincts," "personal habits," techniques, economies, customs, conventionalities.

In all of these activities—among men at least—of animals we know too little to speak—there has been of course from time to time some conscious adaptation; but as systems of conduct they are for the most part, I think, unconscious* activities, the outcome of what is perhaps vaguely but most generally called instinct. Moreover the average man shifts the effort of making the more or less inevitable adaptation upon the expert, taking to himself the rôle of imitation, a rôle of instinct. Into an analysis of instinct I may not go. In this study I have to indicate some of the ways in which dread of novelty, of the unlike or the unusual, has entered into social life; how much our fear of having to change our habits has affected them. To the intolerance or conflict born of this fear or dread I shall but incidentally refer.

This dread or apprehensiveness is both intensified and rendered conspicuous thanks to another instinctive feeling, our instinct of gregariousness. Our longing for the habitual is continually imperilled by our longing for one another. For what is as likely to interfere with our habits as the

---

* Cp. Boas, Franz, *The Mind of Primitive Man*, pp. 221, 228. New York, 1911.

habits of others? Moreover it is personality which most influences personality, a fact curiously more apparent in savage philosophy than in ours.* But the evasiveness induced throughout society by this feature of personality even the modern philosopher has noted. "Does it not seem as if man was of a very sly, elusive nature, and dreaded nothing so much as a full rencontre front to front with his fellow?" queries the great transcendentalist. [1]

That we may gratify both our desire for companionship and our desire to be let alone or rather to go our own gait it is of paramount importance that the personality and habits of others should be like ours. Inevitably different, truly or supposititiously, because of differences of age or sex or environment, the best we can do, we feel,† is to set up barriers between us.

If these social barriers are to remain effectual, it is necessary that the habits they safeguard remain steadfast. For the sake of uniformity the re-

---

* Fear of personal contacts is undisguised in the savage. He is afraid of them because they suggest the unknown of which he is ever afraid, because they offer opportunities to work magic against him, because through them he may "catch" the undesirable qualities of others.

† Is it necessary for me to state that throughout this analysis collective feeling or action is never assumed to be purposeful or deliberative?

striction of personality within the bounds of these habits is also urgent. Hence our insistence that the individual act invariably in conformity with his or her sex, age, class, caste, or nationality, with his or her set part in society. Hence our intolerance of effeminacy or mannishness, of precociousness or immaturity, of the unladylike or the boorish, of inhospitality, of a lack of *esprit de corps* or patriotism. Hence our suspicion of a vagabond and in part our contempt for a derelict; hence the bitterness of our persecution of rebels or minorities, so much more dangerous to our peace of mind than the outlander, however hostile, or than nature, however catastrophic. "Certain forms which all people comply with, and certain arts which all people aim at, hide in some degree the truth* and give a general exterior resemblance to almost everybody."[2] Lord Chesterfield is probably referring to the usages peculiar to the "polite society" of his day,† but is it not along the same lines of conformity or in view of them that many of our wider social forms are drawn, such so-called institutions as the "laws" of hospitality, caste, marriage, the club, the family?

---

* Or personality, let us say.

† That it was closer in essentials to savage society than is our own contemporaneous society our study, I trust, will suggest.

The principle of these institutions is one of grouping or classification. They bring together the like and separate the unlike. Or when for utilitarian or other reasons separation is impracticable, by consistently treating the unlike as representatives of a class and nothing else, by giving them a status, the status of sex, of guest or host, of superior or inferior rank, of wife or husband, of member of a group, a family group, an age group, an occupation group, a local group, etc., in other words by strictly classifying them, they hold them aloof or raise up barriers against them. Applied to the more homogeneous, this classificatory method has also the advantage of precluding any encroachment of personality. It is only as one of the group that you meet its other members, concealing from them whatever in you is not characteristic of the group,* whatever is erratic, changeable, changing, not open to classification, in short whatever is personal.

And so classificatory institutions plan for relationships which will satisfy naturally incompatible tendencies, our gregariousness, and our bent to routine. They do their best too to preclude inter-

---

* It must be because of this concealment that the curious charge of insincerity is so often made against conventionality. It is indeed an extraordinary charge to bring against what is intrinsically so primitive, deep-rooted, and unassumed.

ferences with either tendency. With the nature itself of the interference they preclude, they are primarily not concerned, if concerned at all. That is outside their task. Whatever is individualistic or whatever is likely to blur or break down habit or custom the institutionalized account a social violation—a crime, an immorality, an indignity, an act of selfishness or rudeness, a lack of consideration or respect, bad manners. It is a crime to marry your cousin if your group is exogamous; endogamous, it is immoral not to marry her. Not to be a polygynist in a polygynous society may be a piece of selfishness to your wife; but to be one under monogamy is treating her, she thinks, with indignity. In very many places not to turn your back on your mother-in-law is the height of disrespect; in other places paying no attention to her is a lack of consideration. To pay attention to any woman, even to look at a lady, is conduct unbecoming a gentleman wherever the sexes keep much apart. Generally to treat a woman as if she were a man, a "social superior" as if an equal, a senior as if a contemporary, a guest as if a member of the family, are all serious enough confusions of social distinctions to be called at least bad manners.

Calling unusual behaviour unmannerly is, we

to conform to the conventionalities he fails to admire without losing his self-respect. Because he sees through them, he feels unbound by them. Realities in the past to all perhaps, realities in the present to the undiscerning, to him they are a mere convenience, often, he says, a protection. They smooth his path. "Mere forms," are you not exaggerating their import, denying your sense of humour perhaps, or your class, in taking them so seriously? he is more than likely to prick into you. "Isn't ease under their conventionalities characteristic of truly cultivated persons? As for the others aren't they well enough off, knowing no better?" Shall we meet his query with a figure suggested by his own? To motorists trolley cars are of course a protection. The people who use them leave the roads comparatively unimpeded. Any special joy or sense of adventure in travelling by trolley, to be sure, is rare, and the chances for enjoyment and for seeing the world are better on the whole in a motor car. And yet were the question to arise of making the pleasanter or more adventuresome mode of locomotion available to all, it is quite possible that considerable opposition would appear, opposition not only from the trolley companies and the aristocrats of travel but from the *habitués* of the trolley line themselves. Trolley-ing is so much safer than motoring. These questions of communication or transportation are after all, whether physical or social, questions of democracy, howbeit of a kind of democracy with which the merely political democrat has no great familiarity.

In the following discussions more will be said about safety devices than about the dangers apprehended, about conventionalities than about fear. Nor will I care to press in detail the theory that conventionality of a certain type is ever prompted by fear. Conventionality rests upon an apprehensive state of mind,* but it would be grotesque to try to trace particular conventionalities to particular fears and it would lead one into endless absurdities. I do not take a man's arm to go out to dinner, for example, because I am afraid of tripping over the threshold or falling down stairs, or even, in acknowledgment of weakness, as a gesture of propitiation. But by taking his arm I do raise up an imperceptible kind of barrier between us, a barrier covertly soothing to the sense of disquiet, extremely slight in this circumstance of course, the difference in sex arouses. As a gesture of sex, taking a man's arm is a kind of

---

* That is in society. Conventional ways in an individual do not necessarily betoken, need I say, an apprehensive nature.

inoculation against sex. It divorces sex from personality, and to render sex impersonal is, at times at least, to render it unalarming.

Into all the conventionalities of sex I shall not go, choosing for discussion certain of the more marked conventionalities between the sexes due to sex apprehensiveness. And in general the conventionalities dwelt upon will be those based upon fear, the fear of unlike for unlike. Nor shall I consider all the customs arising out of such fears, limiting myself to customs which modern society* has begun to question and which in one stage of that questioning it is pleased to call, sometimes in justification, sometimes in condemnation, conventionalities.

Customs once generally questioned are apt to change or decay, in other words, conventionalities are naturally short-lived. We might almost define them as customs in decomposition, more or less conscious of their own decay. In fact, many of the conventionalities we are to consider are fast disappearing. For some of my readers therefore a certain amount of detailed description

---

* In this definition savage society is too much identified with its customs to be conventional. Conventionalities are to the life of custom what myths are, it has been argued, to the religious life. Both myths and conventionalities indicate a breaking down in the sense of participation. Cp. Lévy-Bruhl, L., *Les Fonctions Mentales dans les Sociétés Inférieures*, pp. 434 *sq.* Paris, 1910.

seemed necessary. For their sake I hope to be forgiven if to the more conventionally minded I seem at times too expository or too explicit.

" Why in view of their imminent disappearance bestow so much attention upon them?" I may be asked. "Why not take their decease for granted and pass on?" It is a query implying too great a doubt of the value of ethnology in general, or let us say of science, to be met here. But to the reader of ethnological bias may I say that I trust this study will be a contribution, however humble, to his understanding of society.

Fear of change is a part of the state of fear man has ever lived in but out of which he has begun to escape. Civilization might be defined indeed as the steps in his escape. What he now calls conventionality is that part of his system of protection against change he has begun to examine and, his fear lessening, even to forego. If the following discussions are found to substantiate this sociological theory they will serve their purpose—or a part of it.

E. C. P.

New York,
November, 1914.

Fear and Conventionality

I

ON NOT TAKING TO STRANGERS

OUR ways are always more or less endangered, we think, by the Stranger, for his habits or customs differ, we suspect, from ours; probably he has, as it is said in a restricted sense in civilization, different standards of living. Against him we are therefore apt to safeguard ourselves. When we can, we avoid him. We stay away or we run away from him or we keep him away from us.

"I don't want to go there," demurs a son or a daughter. "I don't know any of those fellows," —"I don't know the other girls; I won't have a good time." "A Fijian cannot be comfortable," we are told, "with a stranger at his heels"*; and will not an acquaintance sometimes tell us that

---

* Williams, Th., *Fiji and the Fijians*, i, 133. London, 1858. Because he lives ever in fear of his life, writes Williams; but his fear of the stranger may be, I surmise, more general.

he or she takes not easily to strangers or does not like to meet them? Have we not all known persons too shy their life long to go with pleasure "into society"? To feel at ease in any society is a mark of the caste of whom gallantry is demanded. But even a gentleman, if he actually knows something against a stranger, perhaps that he is an abolitionist or an ex-convict, an I. W. W. or a militant suffragist, may "refuse to meet" him. He would not be seen with him or shake his hand or sit down to table with him. He gives him a wide berth. When he passes, a gentleman or at any rate a lady will look the other way.

"Our immediate impulse may be to look the other way when any person at whom we have been looking becomes aware of us," remarks William James[1] of a common experience. Staring, we say, is impolite. And, unless we are actresses or social leaders, for no reason we can express we resent being stared at. Even the tourist minds it. Looking at a person's face, says a Chinaman, shows pride. Not even the Son of Heaven looks at a person "above his collar." "The ruler of a state looks at him a little lower, a great officer, on a line with his heart," and five paces away an ordinary officer does not look at him at all.[2]

On the other hand, to look a stranger in the eye is sometimes taken to be a test of character or of gentle breeding—when it is not black magic.* John Trott, the typical English boor, is described by Lord Chesterfield as never looking people in the face, and many a child besides Lord Chesterfield's little godson[3] has to be taught to look at the person he shakes hands with or addresses.

> "Who spekithe to the in any maner place,
>   Rudely, cast not thyn ye adowne,
>   But with a sadde chiere loke hym in the face."[4]

Nor is it only English children who cast down their eyes or look askance at the stranger. The Aki-kúyus, a vigorous tribe immigrant in British East Africa, call the tribe of timid dwarfs they dispossessed *Mai tho ma chi-á-na*, "the people that look at you as a child would."[5] On Dr. Felkin's first appearance in the Court of Uganda, so frightened were the royal children by his white face that they rushed away.

Even less than a black face causes our children sometimes to rush away and hide from the new-

---

* Simple people, as we know, often carry charms against the evil eye. Natives of Borneo have been known to fear that Europeans by looking at them would make them ill. (Crawley, E., *The Mystic Rose*, p. 114. London and New York, 1902.)

comer. When Byron was a boy he used to jump out of the drawing-room window to escape callers.[6] We know grown-ups "whose first impulse when the doorbell rings, or a visitor is suddenly announced, is to scuttle out of the room so as not to be 'caught.'"[7] So fearful of strangers are some of the timid jungle tribes of India that the mere sight of one puts to flight a whole community.[8] When the Regent of Java paid a visit with Dutch officials to the capital of the Baduwis in the almost inaccessible mountains of the island, all the people fled the place never to return.[9] While digging up a prehistoric community house in New Mexico, I one day asked the Pueblo Indian at work with me why his ancestors had moved away from the place. "Because they knew the White Men were coming," he naïvely answered, betraying his own point of view in being so well satisfied that his answer was adequate. The very primitive Vedda of Ceylon once* traded with the Sinhalese on a strictly credit basis. Putting down his share in the deal somewhere on the edge of his tribal land, the Vedda trader would return in a few days to get the axes and

---

* The "silent trade" is no longer practised, although the Veddas still avoid strangers for everything but barter. (Seligmann, C. G. and B. J., *The Veddas*, pp. 93-4. Cambridge, 1911.)

arrow-points the unknown Sinhalese had left in payment.[10]

The Veddas elude not only their fellow islanders; they run away from their own ghosts, deserting their cave homes whenever anyone in them dies.[11] Australian Blackfellows show their fear of the dead in the same way, and so does many another savage horde. Obviously, through their new experiences, the dead have become alien to the living and formidable. Is it not mostly for this reason that anyone, anywhere, is afraid of ghosts, and does his best to avoid meeting them?

Reassuring as running away from ghosts or "total foreigners" or unexpected callers may be, flight in itself breaks down habits and requires new adaptations—unless people are at any rate nomadic or semi-nomadic. And even nomads may return to once deserted spots—after the danger is past, when the Stranger, living or dead, is supposed to have departed.*

With a more settled way of living it is naturally more convenient to keep the Stranger at a distance than to run away from him. On the theory

*But he is apt to remain. The fact that primitive nomads (hunters and fishers in distinction to stockraisers) live in inaccessible places, in mountains or on islands, is evidence that he comes to stay.

that the intrusion of a White Man would cause
the death of their king, the Malagasy of Mahafly
closed the whole of their country to Europeans. [12]
When Speke was travelling in Central Africa,
the natives of one of the villages he wished to stop
at shut their doors against him, never before having
seen a White Man or such tin boxes as he carried. [13]
Recently on a stormy walk in Long Island a
"foreign born American" shut her door in my
face when I asked for shelter, a not uncommon
experience for the "Dago" tramp at the mercy
of the New England housewife.   In 1840 China
excluded the   British — forever.   To-day the
United States excludes the Chinese; Russia excludes Hebrews; Hayti, Syrians; Canada, Hindus.
And almost every society exorcises its ghosts—
after allowing them a reasonable time to depart
in, perhaps a few days, perhaps months or years.*

Sometimes ghosts are allowed to stay on inde-
finitely if they keep to the quarters assigned them,
but if they walk unscrupulously they are sure to
be laid.   The live Stranger may be similarly
treated.   To Calais early in the seventeenth

---

*The living are not always treated with equal consideration.
A year or two ago in enforcing its exclusion act retroactively,
Hayti refused to allow a Syrian resident who had been away
on business to land merely to close his house and wind up his
affairs.

century outsiders were admitted, but any
stranger "of what Nation so-ever" who was
"taken walking by himself about the greene of
the towne" was imprisoned until he paid a fine.[14]
In the medieval city of Europe the Jew was segregated in a pale; in Russia the ghetto is still extant
and the right of domicile is withheld from Jews
in more than three-fourths of the country. Until
1858 they were kept from qualifying for the House
of Commons; in the United States clubs or hotels
may be closed to them or under the management
of a fashionable opera-house they may be kept off
the list of box-holders. Europeans and Americans
in the Chinese Treaty Ports have had to live in the
Foreign Concessions. In Uganda no European
was allowed to live anywhere in the country outside of the capital.[15] In parts of the United
States negroes are still kept out of schools, tenements, cars, voting booths, playhouses, and beach
pavilions.

II

TRAVELLERS

TO go out among strangers, to be a man of the
world, to travel, has always taken more or
less courage and considerable inducements—wives,
treasure, slaves, foreign-made goods, foreign alli-
ances, the favours of the gods, lands to be claimed
or seas charted, a Golden Fleece, a Sacred Tomb,
a North-west Passage. Of course if, like raider or
sailor or crusader, or like the modern tourist, you
seek out only compatriots when you travel,* you
feel comparatively secure, a feeling they whose
business it is to exploit the tourist fully appreciate;
but a solitary stranger in a strange land† has

---

* "Most of the English who travel converse only with each
other," writes Lord Chesterfield. (Letter VIII.) Travelling
North Americans also flock together, except when one suspects
the other of being "common." But even this suspicion is not
entertained by the hypergregarious Cook's tourist.

† Particularly a woman. In primitive groups women rarely
if ever travel alone. Even in the United States there is a prejudice against employing women as commercial travellers, and
not long ago in New York City certain hotels declined to take
in women travelling alone. On the other hand, savage women

ever had to have an adventurous spirit. Realization of the perils he faces is apt to find ceremonial expression. In his behalf sacrifices are offered to the gods or prayers said or he is himself the recipient of farewell gifts. He is provided with amulets or letters of introduction or wished a *"bon voyage"* or *"good luck."* As he sets off he is on the lookout for omens, and often an unfavourable omen checks his start. There are days too, he learns, when he had better not start at all— Sunday, Tuesday, and Friday in the Soudan,[1] Friday among us, and Friday, too, in Persia, if western bound.[*] In Persia a kinsman holds a Koran over a traveller's head as he crosses the threshold.[2] Elsewhere too he is "seen off." In Northern Albania he is accompanied for a mile or two on his journey by his relatives, returning to them, on leave-taking, the gold and silver

---

are sometimes sent on dangerous ambassadorial missions on the ground that they run less risk of attack than men. It is fear of the unusual, a fear greater in women I surmise than in men, that has deterred women from travel rather than any definite fear of attack.

[*] "On Saturday and Monday, O my brother, it is best not to proceed towards the East. From the West, danger impends on Sunday and Friday. On Tuesday and Wednesday beware lest thy destiny leads thee towards the North. And when Thursday's sun hath risen, never direct thy course to the South." (Binning, R. B. M., *A Journal of Two Years' Travel in Persia, Ceylon, etc.*, ii, 246. London, 1857.)

earrings he has had to take from a jar of magic
water.[3] On setting out to the East Coast the
Wanyamwesi of the Soudan smear their cheeks
with a kind of meal porridge[4] or else have their
medicine-men spit it over them,[5] just as before
going to Europe we might have our hair cut or
buy a "travelling suit." No Moslem ever travels
without taking with him his grave clothes.[*]
"Does not travel itselfe put in minde of the
slippernes, uncertainty and shortnesse of this
life?" queries a Christian exponent of wayfaring
advantages.[6]

While the traveller is away, prayers are said
for his "safe return" or charms performed. The
family of an Aeneze Arab may vow to place ostrich
feathers, on his return, on one of the poles of the
tent.[7] "Guard him," prays the Christian, "from
the dangers of the sea, from sickness, from the vio-
lence of enemies, and from every evil to which he
may be exposed." The Catholic friends of the
aeroplanist make their supplications for his safety
to Saint Anthony, richest of saints in the *ex-voti*
of grateful travellers. To the Goddess of Fire
and the Sacred Skulls the old men of the Ainu

---

* Wilson and Felkin, ii, 308. No doubt an exaggeration.
Cp.·Burckhardt, J. L., *Notes on the Bedouins and Wahábys*, p. 160.
London, 1830.

make libations of *saké* and renew their offerings
of willow shavings. "Oh, ye Gods," they pray,
"our sons have gone away . . . we think of
them much, oh do ye watch over them and prosper
them . . . and bring them safely home."[8]

Back "safe and sound," the traveller is "met."
When a Blackfellow of some importance approaches
a camp, "the inmates close in with raised arms,
as if in defence; then the person of note rushes
at them, making a faint blow as if to strike them,
they warding it off with their shields; immediately
after they embrace him and lead him into the
camp, where the women bring him food."[9] Somewhat like scenes of mock scrimmage may be witnessed among us at the landing of a Transatlantic
liner or on the arrival of trains from Albany,
let us say, or Washington. But even less distinguished travellers than English militants or French
actresses or American politicians are "met" to
be welcomed or congratulated. "I am glad you
got back safely," says the polite American to his
acquaintance returned from a trip abroad.* "Have
you journeyed in safety?" ask the Awemba, ex-
pecting the stereotyped answer: "Yes, God has

* "After a return from Europe," I read in an American book
on etiquette, "it is proper to call in person, or to leave a card."
(*Manners and Social Usages*, p. 7. New York and London, 1907.)

spoken to us on the way."[10]   "*Kulika lutalo*," "I congratulate you on your safe return," says one M'ganda to another. "*Awo*," "Thank you." "*Kulika nyo*," "I congratulate you very much." "*Awo*."[11]

To those who have been solicitous the returned traveller makes presents—to the prayerful elders in Japan among the Ainu, to his *yutchin** among the Dieri[12] of Australia, to friends and kindred among us. Among us, although these souvenirs of travel are still provided for in our customs regulations, they are no longer a matter of course; but I remember the time when no one ever thought of returning from abroad without a present for every member of his family or household. One of my acquaintances on her first "trip-to-Europe" brought back a French hat to her cook.

The returned traveller has prestige. He is given a public reception or fêted in private. The neighbours want to hear his yarns—even if they do not always believe them. His friends—if they are sufficiently devoted—take an interest in the photographs he has made or bought, or if they are

---

* A friend who collects presents for him while he is away. To remember his promise to bring presents to his *yutchin*, a Dieri traveller has a string of flax or human hair tied around his neck, having no handkerchief to knot or ring to change to another finger.

Ainu listen by the hour to the stories he chants to them.[13] Among the Dieri after his news is whispered to the relatives and friends sitting around, it is repeated in a loud voice to the whole camp.[14] Among us he is interviewed by newspaper reporters and the public reads his travel book. He is noted thereafter as a man who has been around the world or who has visited its remote or wild or holy places.

The traveller to holy places, the pilgrim, acquires special prestige or merit. The Moslem who has been to Mecca is entitled to wear a green turban and tunic for the rest of his life[15]—has he not compelled the gods by his pilgrimage to forgive his sins and grant his requests? For like reasons the medieval Christian who had reached Jerusalem was venerated;—in those days to discount the advantages of a pilgrimage to the Holy Land one had to be as arrogant of soul as Frederick the Second. To other lords of the earth pilgrimage and even travel for secular ambitions have brought prestige. Did not India add to Alexander's reputation, Gaul and England to Cæsar's, Rome to Alaric's, Africa and South America to Roosevelt's?

To the chief's forerunner, the medicine-man or priest, travel is also one of the sources of prestige he usually avails himself of. In savage tribes he

is the foremost or only traveller; as a Buddhist
monk he was among the first to journey from India
to Alexandria, from China to India, or as a Catholic friar from Europe to Tibet, to Japan, to the
New World. In Africa the Christian missionary
is still the first to shoulder the White Man's bur-
den, and a year or so ago the Bab himself visited
the United States.

But the medicine-man goes even beyond the
ends of the earth. One of his greatest professional
assets is his story of his trip to Ghost-land, to the
Other World, to the Home of the Gods, or to the
Throne of God. And medicine-men almost always claim to have the power to travel away from
their own body and incarnate themselves in other
persons or in animals. Moreover they have only
to predict with assurance about their own existence after death, the boundary line of the Unknown Country, to found a cult, sometimes tran-
sient, sometimes, as in Christianity, abiding.

To many peoples Ghost-land is a fixed place.
Ghosts are supposed either to linger about their
old haunts or to travel to a locality more or less
well mapped-out. Their life goes on with as
little break as possible.* Death is but a journey,

* This continuity theory of life after death probably accounts
in part for the comparative indifference to death of the peoples

and so like other wayfarers the dying expect to
have ceremonies performed for them to lessen
the embarrassments or dangers bound to beset
them. A whale's tooth was put in the hand of a
Fijian to throw at a pandanus tree and thereby
assure the dispatch to him of his wife.[16] The
Greek was given a gold piece as a tip to
his ghostly ferryman. A pillow of soil from
Jerusalem is put under the encoffined head of a
Jew dying in Eastern Europe to save him from
rolling underground, afflicted by the angels, all
the way to Jerusalem, a journey taking forty
years.[17] In the coffin of a Yezidi Kurd are placed
silver and a stick wherewith to bribe or beat his
postmortem catechists into letting him into
Heaven.[18] Entombed with a Chinaman are a
miniature sedan chair of bamboo or paper, paper
models of chairmen, and paper money to pay them
with; and to furnish *Lû-in* or a "passport for
travelling from this life to the next"* is a specialty
of Chinese priests.[19] A *viaticum* is provided for the

who hold it. But even a believer in a religion preaching reward
and punishment after death can urge us to "prepare our life
. . . to that last and heavenly pilgrimage by the custom of . . .
travels here on earth." (Coryat, i, 148.)
 * Such a passport the Greek Church, it is said, once furnished
a deceased Russian grand duchess. (Parsons, Elsie Clews, *The
Old-Fashioned Woman*, p. 317. New York, 1913.)

Catholic, and in Italy in the seventeenth century it was his privilege to be buried in the cowl of a Franciscan friar, it having the virtue, it was believed, of remitting a third part of his sins.[20] Masses are still said by Catholics to expedite the journey of their beloved dead from Purgatory to Paradise. Except in the most modern cults, enough food and drink are almost always provided at a funeral to last the departing spirit through the beginning at least of his journey.

The way in which the dying set off is considered almost everywhere important. In New Guinea a dying man has to be propped up in a squatting position, his hands lying in his lap.[21] "I want for nothing but to die in the correct way," said Confucius.[22] Making a pious ending, dying placidly, serene to the last, meeting death with a smile, are auspicious and notable circumstances to most Christian biographers. The fact that indifference or apathy is the characteristic mood at death they persistently overlook. Death-bed scenes are essential, they think, to their story. But in real life the dying are supposed to be "seen off" too.* Neighbours and

* Except when the fear their departure excites has overwhelmed other feelings. Then they are taken ceremonially out-of-doors or borne away from home and sometimes left to die alone. Much of corpse taboo is amply explained by dread of the unusual.

relatives* are sent for to gather around them
in prayer or for a last word, and great significance attaches to their farewells or blessings.
By the Jews of the Near East they are given messages to carry to the patriarchs and the pro-
phets, and distinguished Rabbis are entrusted
with letters in their coffins to deceased friends.[23]
African potentates have had the habit of de-
spatching slaves to carry messages to their dead
forebears or to give them the latest mundane
news. Like other travellers the dead have prestige.
Sometimes more attention is paid to them than
they ever received in life, and they arouse
deeper feelings of fear or affection or pity.
Their wishes are considered, their failings overlooked or even respected. Particularly impressive
is he who sets off on the long journey of his
own will, because he merely wants a change.
To some communities a suicide appears so
potent a ghost that his coffin is nailed down or
stakes are driven through his corpse or he is denied burial in consecrated ground. His act is
stirring or shocking—to those in the habit of liv-

* A Vedda who was not summoned to the death-bed of his
father-in-law would be as much put out at being overlooked as
one of us under like circumstances. (Seligmann, *The Veddas*,
p. 115.)

2

ing—and he becomes the recipient of virulent abuse or, more rarely, of unmeasured praise. The lack of fear shown in his voluntary departure may inspire admiration, a wondering, pitying, uncertain kind of admiration. And yet has he not shirked every conventionality of dying, alike in theory and in practice? Has he not been inconsiderate of those he leaves behind, sometimes to the extent of not even taking leave of them? Is he not taking a journey uncompelled by circumstance and without any very definite purpose, not even giving the wonted assurance that he will be back soon?—unless he has killed himself, as the Chinaman sometimes does, the better to qualify himself to take a revenge.

The feeling aroused in us by suicide, whether admiration or antagonism, betrays the attitude of fear we take towards the Last Journey. Only more intense, it is the same attitude adopted in the past towards all journeying. It is because of our apprehensiveness of the unknown besetting travel and of the changes incident to it, that we are so scrupulous to say good-bye and see people off, that we are anxious until we see them again, and that we congratulate them or perform ceremonies of welcome on their return—on their return to the certainties and stabilities of home.

III

HOSPITALITY: THE GUEST

WELL aware of the attitude towards him of the man who does not know him, an understanding traveller, a man of parts, will be adaptable. "When you are in Rome, do as the Romans do," is a counsel of protective colouration, as it were. "A man of the world must, like the chameleon, be able to take every different hue," writes Lord Chesterfield.* "To avoyde envye and to keepe companye pleasauntlye with every man, let him do whatsoever other men do,"¹ is the advice given to the ideal courtier. In courts and out of them much of the etiquette of hospitality is based indeed on the theory of a new-comer's conformity. When Dr. Felkin appeared one day in the royal court of Uganda with his hair cut, King Mutesa was so flattered,† a shaven

*Letter XXX. None understood better the value of conformity in the art of self-protection.

† On another occasion Felkin was less happy. That his guest might be properly served the King offered him the sum of eighteen wives. Felkin declined the present. "Why not take them?"

crown being a court fashion, that he sent his guest a goat.[2] It was quite natural for Batchelor's Ainu hosts to ask him to seal his brotherhood with them by having his ears pierced like theirs for a piece of red flannel.[3] It was natural too for the new-found friends of Zeyneb Hanoum, the *désenchantée* who escaped from Constantinople to Paris, to send her hats. "Hardly a day passes but someone sends us a hat," she writes.[4] She had twenty.

A guest is expected not to boast of his own gods, or at least not to decry his host's—a breach of hospitality sometimes greatly to the discredit of the missionary. Were he more mannerly he would be more reticent and might even, like other guests, go to church with the family* and join in family prayers† and in saying whatever grace

---

asked the King. "Haven't you any women in your country?" "Yes, but we allow only one wife, and we do not make presents of women wholesale." Then the King fell into a rage. "You come here and say all men are brothers," he cried, "and that your God loves us as well as you, and yet you think yourselves too good to live as we do. Ugh!" (Wilson and Felkin, ii, 17.)

* "A mannerly guest will cheerfully accompany the family to their church, even tho' it be of a different faith from her own; and she will listen respectfully to the sermon, and refrain from ungracious criticism of the choir or the minister." (Morton, A. H., *Etiquette*, pp. 123–4. Philadelphia, 1911.)

† If the hour of family worship "is mentioned to guests, their presence is obligatory." (*The Complete Hostess*, p. 284. New York, 1906.)

was usual among those he was visiting. Even his
colleague in civilization waits to be asked to say
grace when he is dining out.* And as a rule he is
careful not to introduce religious topics at the
dinner table. In fact, to be quite safe, no mannerly guest will mention religion at all.† Use
"no freedom with others about their religious
sentiments," wrote Dr. Gregory to his daughters.[5]
Politics we know is also at times an eschewed
topic of conversation. These rules of polite intercourse are becoming somewhat out of date in the
United States, perhaps because in this country
neither church nor state excites enough interest
as a rule to provoke heated discussion and to be,
therefore, a dangerous subject of conversation.
Still their critics are apt to show enough consideration for an interlocutor to preface criticism
with: "You are not a Catholic, are you?"—"I
don't know what your politics are, but," etc.
The Chinese rule on the whole seems safer. "If
the host have not put some question, the visitor
should not begin the conversation."[6]

A well-behaved guest should be very careful

---

* Asking an ecclesiastical guest to say grace is nowadays a
striking instance, by the way, of how hard a host will try to make
a guest feel at home.

† Nor uninvited attend family prayers. His presence "would
be an intrusion." (*The Complete Hostess*, p. 284.)

in making known his wants or tastes. They may be unlike those of his host, and his host may therefore be disconcerted by not being able to provide for them. It is a little hard on your hostess to tell her you never can sleep in a light room when her house is neither built nor furnished to shut out the sun. Greatly mortified must have been the hostess of the guest who exclaimed when the roast was offered to her: "My grandmother Jones never could eat lamb, and I never can."[7] No guest should run the risk of letting her hostess think that partiality for a darkened bedroom or for French chops or partridge is evidence on her part of a superior taste. However tacit, comparisons to the disadvantage of a host should never be indulged in.

Obviously the considerate guest will eat or drink whatever is set before him. "A guest should not rinse his mouth with spirits till the host has gone over all the dishes," prescribes one of the Chinese classics.[8] Whether hungry or not, the Iroquois guest was bound to taste of every dish presented to him and say, "*Hz-ne-ä'-weh*," "I thank you."[9] In many other circles in the United States a guest is expected to taste at least of every dish served, par-

ticularly the soup;* and dishes are pressed upon
him or as something "special" called to his attention. Having in self-preservation to decline
them, he will at least make elaborate excuses for
his failure of appetite. Scrupulous to avoid the
merest suggestion of criticism, he will take the
entire blame upon himself. To pointed questions, he says that he likes dark meat as well as
white, the well cooked as well as the underdone†;
he drinks his tea or coffee "just as it comes"; as
for his breakfast, "whatever you have will do for
me," he genially responds.

> "Bot prayse thi fare, wer-so-ever thou be,
>   Fore be it gode or be it badde,
>   Yu gud worth it muste be had."[10]

Not to eat what is given to him may be impolitic
or even imprudent in a guest. Among the Steins,
a Shan tribe of Siam, unless a visitor eats *all* that
is set before him and drinks through his bamboo
tube out of the common cup, he is liable to be
knifed.[11] There was a time when "challenged"

---

* "If soup is helped first, take some, whether you like it or
not; . . . sip a few spoonfuls, if you do no more." (Farrar,
Mrs. John, *The Young Lady's Friend*, p. 343. New York,
1841.)

† And yet it may be more polite "to make a choice, whether
you have a preference or not; because it is most agreeable to the
carver, to have the matter decided by you." (*Ib.*, p. 344.)

at table to take wine no American guest would
dare decline.   Even a lady was supposed to "accept the challenge graciously."   "Choose one of
the wines named to you," she was told, "look full
at the gentleman you are to drink with, then drop
your eyes as you bow your head to him, and lift
the glass to your lips, whether you drink a drop
or not.   If challenged a second time, accept, and
have a drop added to your glass, and bow as
before."[12]

In particulars unrelated to the table a guest will
endeavour too not to disturb the family habits or
the household routine.   He will "interfere as little
as possible with the regular avocations of the
family."[13]   He must "never be in the way."[14]   A
New Guinea guest is expected not to hang around
the circle of stones where his host lounges to gossip.[15]   Although an American guest "should aim
to feel and act as though the interests and pleasures
of the family were his own,"[16] he must not treat
the servants, he is told, or any of his host's things,
as if they belonged to him.[17]

Nor is a guest expected to ask questions as a
rule about the household machinery.   It is supposed in fact to be more or less invisible to him—
or shall we change the sex for a moment and say, to
her?   Parts of the house she may never enter, and

in general she must make her approach with care.
If possible she will inform her hostess in advance
of the hour of her arrival, knowing that her hostess
wishes not only to pay her the compliment of
meeting her but that no hostess likes to be taken
unexpectedly. Should she fail "to make the
train or boat by which she is expected, she should
at once wire or long-distance 'phone her hostess,
explaining the mishap, and suggesting that no
trouble be taken about hitching up to meet her,
but that she will endeavour to get to her friend's
house in a depot hack or hired conveyance."[18]
But even where there are no postal or telegraph
or long-distance telephone facilities in the country, visitors are careful not to take their hosts
unaware. A Blackfellow would not think of
suddenly breaking in upon the privacy of the
horde he is about to visit. He warns it of his arrival by building a fire or even a series of little
fires some distance off.[19] Within sight of the
camp, he sits down waiting to be invited in.[20]
Throughout the Orient, it is good manners to
send on your servant to announce your coming.
Among grandees heralds have ever been important
functionaries.

On entering a man's house or room a visitor
should also announce himself or let himself be an-

nounced. We knock on the door or send in our
visiting card. As he approaches a M'ganda calls
out, "*Abemuno mwemulit?*" "You of the place,
are you there?"[21]   A quarter of a mile away from
an encampment a Vedda stops and shouts and
does not go on until an answering shout is heard.[22]
Nearing a house an Ainu makes a prolonged
guttural sound—"he-he-he-he-hem."[23]   A Chinaman raises his voice.[24]   Nor would a Chinaman
go directly up the steps to his host. "I, so-
and-so," he says to the "officer of communication,"
"earnestly wish to see him."[25]   Even within the
house when about to enter the door, he knows
"he must keep his eyes cast down," nor, having
to look up or down, should he turn his head.[26]

A guest has to be careful in general about his
movements through the house. With us he is
expected to go through a doorway first, his host
holding back and sometimes saying, "After you"
or "You first." In China he is invited to go
first, but he is expected to refuse firmly, and then
to enter together with his host. Having entered,
the host moves to the right to the steps on the
east and the guest to the left to the steps on the
west. "They then offer to each other the precedence in going up, but the host commences first.
They bring their feet together on every step,"

the host moving his right foot first, the guest his
left.[27] A Comanche host is as offended if his
guest* does not pass through his lodge and take
the seat pointed out to him[28] as would be a Chinaman if his guest did not sit facing the south[29]
or a New England housewife if her visitor did not
come in at the front door and sit down in the
rocking-chair in the "parlor."

Of course guests are not expected to stray about
or explore. Visiting Blackfellows are required always to reach the place assigned them in the camp
by going behind the huts and not in front.[30] In
Santal houses the "stranger's seat" is outside the
door.[31] Strangers are not allowed on one of the
verandahs of the Kakhyen tribesman's house,†
and when Parker was travelling in the Kakhyen
country with the British inspectors of the Burma-
Chinese boundary he was never invited into the
back region of the Kakhyen house and to his
chagrin he could get no idea of what went on
there. Mrs. Farrar advised young ladies to save
the domestics of their hostess unnecessary steps by

---

*The Eskimo guest is similarly conducted by his host to the
place set for him. (Egede, Hans, *A Description of Greenland*, p.
126. London, 1818.)

† For a stranger to enter by the back door would be not only
very impolite, but an outrage upon the tutelary spirit of the
house. (Colquhoun, ii, 348.)

waiting on themselves *providing* their hostess had "no objection" to guests entering her kitchen.[32] I have seen American housewives of a later period show much annoyance at guests "poking about" in their pantries—even when introduced into them by younger members of the family.

A modern nursery a guest enters only on invitation, and very young members of the family are apt at any rate to be secluded from guests. I have been on week-end parties near New York without learning even the number of the children in the family. Elsewhere a guest may be kept in ignorance not only of the offspring of the host but of his wife or wives. In Uganda, for example, wives as well as children eat in private when the head of the household is entertaining a guest.[33] The family life is in fact usually kept away or protected from a guest—sometimes on the plea, a valid plea too, that he is protected from it. "Before an honored visitor we should not shout even at a dog," reads the *Li Ki.* Nor when declining food, the Chinese teaching on hospitality continues, should one spit.[34] When Blackfellows are hosts to a visiting horde silence reigns at night in the camp, for it would be a breach of etiquette to indulge in the

usual night squabbles.[35] "Company manners"
are "put on" for a guest.

Then he, or more particularly she, is "entertained."[*] People are asked to "meet" her[†]—
perhaps the easiest of methods of keeping a
guest occupied and rendering her innocuous.

On the other hand a guest must be very
particular about bringing outsiders into the
family, particularly, I am told, if the hostess
is a woman of fashion.[‡] At any rate for a
girl "to take the liberty of receiving a man without asking permission of her hostess would be
unpardonable."[36] Having given her permission,
a hostess will welcome her guest's caller, "but
after a little withdraw, on some pretext or other,
to an adjoining room, returning to take leave of

[*] "If the guest be a young girl, she [the hostess] will arrange
for a girls' luncheon, a small dance, or card party, the latter
being an easy way of entertaining either old or young, but not
to be considered, of course, if her visitor has no knowledge of,
or even liking for, that form of amusement, to say nothing of
religious scruples against it. " (*The Complete Hostess*, p. 280.)

The Eskimos spend whole days and nights in singing and
dancing to entertain their guests from abroad. (Egede, p. 163.)

[†] "The hostess will naturally desire her friends to show her
some attention." (*The Complete Hostess*, p. 280.)

[‡] "If the hostess be a very fashionable woman and the visitor
decidedly not so, it is . . . vulgar to make one's friend who may
be a guest in the house a sort of entering wedge for an acquaintance; a card should be left, but unaccompanied by any request
to see the lady of the house." (*Manners and Social Usages*, p.
16.)

the visitor ere he departs."[37] This ceremony is prompted in part at least by the theory that a kind of indivisibility exists between hostess and guest. It is rude, for example, not to leave a card on a guest when you are calling on her hostess or *vice versa* on the hostess when your call is for the guest,[38] or, again, to invite to a party a guest without her hostess or a hostess without her guest.[39] Nor, "unless the guest be a frequent visitor, or a sensible one who insists upon it," will any hostess "leave her for an entire evening"—at least "without providing something for her amusement or entertainment."[40]

If by chance company manners break down during a visit—there may be sickness in the family or some crisis in family affairs may occur—the least a guest can do is to send a message to himself calling him away on important business. A letter or telegram is necessary for two reasons— it enables him to continue ignoring the family crisis, and it keeps him from violating the general rule of hospitality of not leaving before the appointed time—at least without an acceptable excuse and a ready response to the customary query—"Must you really go?" With the best of intentions or manœuvres it may be impossible for a guest to be blind to what is going

on. Besides he may by the merest accident
open the door of the family skeleton's closet.   In
such case he is expected of course after he leaves
not to "violate the privacy of the family."   He
is at any rate expected not to talk much about
his hosts, and certainly not to criticise them.
Gossip about their "peculiarities" or about the
"family imperfections" is in very bad taste.[41]
"Whatever you may have remarked to the disadvantage of your friends, whilst sharing their
hospitality, should never transpire through your
means."[42]

In fact, once you have broken bread with a man
or taken a drink with him, you are in many places
under an obligation not to give him away as well
as not to kill him.   Hence not to accept a drink
from a man may be highly significant.   It may
mean that you have designs against him.*   On
the other hand it may also mean that you believe he has designs against you.†   The practice of "treating" has deeper roots than at first
appears, and that anti-treat reform which origi-

---

* This notion may account for the excess expected of guests at
table.

† The Papuans of Humboldt Bay would not touch the water
offered them by their European visitors. (Crawley, p. 157.)
A little boy I know refuses to eat from another's plate or drink
from his glass.   "I'd get his taste," says he.

nated some time ago in New York, a harder road to travel. Indeed to realize the ambitiousness of his campaign, the anti-treat New Yorker should be familiar with an incident alleged to have occurred at the original landing of the Dutch on his island. It is said that the Manhattan Indians were drawn up in a circle to receive the Dutch captain, to their awe-struck eyes a great red-habited Manitou, and that the first act of the Dutchman was to take a drink from a cup of rum and then to offer the cup to the chief standing next to him. The chief smells it and passes it on, and so it passes from hand to hand without being tasted, until it reaches a brave who is not only a great warrior but a man of ideas. He at once warns the company of the impropriety of returning the cup full. To follow the example of the Manitou and take a drink will please him, not to drink will annoy him, perhaps enrage him. He himself will drink whatever the consequences. Better for one to die than for an entire tribe to be destroyed. So speaking he bids the assembly farewell and gulps down the whole contents* of the cup. [43]—Here was one who needed no books

---

* Needless to say the act of devotion temporarily incapacitates the brave. Notwithstanding, he is soon able to ask for another drink and to encourage his friends to drink with him.

on manners to teach him the proper relation between host and guest! Is it because we have
forgotten the reasoning of the savage that we
ourselves have to depend on these publications?

IV

HOSPITALITY: THE HOST

THE ill-will of a guest is everywhere dreaded, partly because as a stranger he has, like the Dutch captain, a quasi-supernatural character, or, in the words of the Daghestan highlanders, he is "a man from God,"[1] and partly because despite barriers his contact with his host[2] has been close enough to allow the fear of contagious magic to be entertained. It becomes very important, therefore, not only to please a guest, but to arouse and strengthen in him a sense of obligation. And so a host offers a guest his best.* If he is an Anglo-Saxon he opens a bottle of his best old wine. If he is a M'ganda he gives him a pinch of salt, a rarity in Uganda.[3] No matter how indifferent a Mattoal Indian may be to

---

* Or in rare instances declines to offer him anything. At Pululaa in the Solomon Islands, guests have to bring their food with them; it is always a "Dutch treat" because of the belief that a guest could work mysteriously upon a host through a morsel of his food. (Crawley, p. 127.)

the wants of his family, with his guest he will
share his last crust—or shred of dried salmon. [4]
A rich Afghan chief is satisfied with nothing less
than the slaying of a sheep when he receives a
distinguished guest—as Pennell, the medical missionary, once appreciated to his cost. Having
arrived at a village late one evening, he was well
entertained by the chief's son, the chief being
away, and given a good supper of fowl. After
a wearisome day, he was soon fast asleep,
only to be aroused at one A.M., to partake of
the sheep the returning chief had had killed
when he learned that only a fowl had been
offered to his guest. Such a lack of hospitality,
protested the chief, would be everlastingly to his
discredit. [5]

Women as well as food and drink are not un-
commonly at the command of a guest. Marco
Polo tells us that to preclude this form of hospitality an enlightened ruler of the Chinese province of
Camul ordered the people to provide public hostel-
ries. They provided them for three years, a period, as it turned out for them, of poor harvests and
general misfortune. So they sent a grand present
to their ruler, begging him to let them return to
their good old custom, by reason of which alone
their gods bestowed upon them all the good things

they were possessed of.[6]   Whatever the motives, Eskimos, Blackfellows, and several other peoples lend their wives to their guests.   Even where this so-called sexual hospitality is not in vogue, a man sometimes feels it incumbent upon him not to join the circle of his wife's callers at tea-time, and generally not to monopolise her attention when other men are present.

Guests are served first—except to the extent a host feels called upon to prove himself innocent of murderous or of magical intent.   In the Banks' Islands the host takes the first bite to take any risk upon himself.[7]   With us a well-trained butler always pours a little of the wine into the host's glass before serving it to the guests, just as among the Krumen[8] or the Makololo[9] at a palm-wine or beer drinking-party the housewife takes the first drink—to take off the "fetish" or to prove the beverage unpoisoned.*

Guests are given the most honourable or comfortable seat,—the east or sacred end of the hearth among the Ainu,[10] the *sadr* or floor space opposite the door end of the room in Persia,[11] the camels' pack-saddles piled at the back of the tent or in

---

* The Fors of the Soudan give their guest another form of assurance by offering him his first drink in a cup of rhinoceros horn, such cups having the virtue of betraying whatever may be poisoning their contents. (Wilson and Felkin, ii, 275.)

the middle* among the Aenezes,¹² the sofa or rocking-chair with us.

To be quite safe, no matter how hospitable he intends to be, a host may receive his guest with an immunity-giving rite. As soon as a stranger appears in some of the Arab villages of Morocco, he is given water or, if he is an important person, milk to drink. If he subsequently misbehaves himself, this drink, he knows, will make his knees swell up and keep him from running away. Other Arabs welcome a guest by pouring on his head a cup of melted butter¹³; the South African Hereros give him a cup of milk,¹⁴ the Awemba of Rhodesia a gourd of beer,¹⁵ his American host or hostess a cocktail or a cup of tea.

When a Wemba knows the path his guest is taking he always sends his children out to meet him.¹⁶ A careful American host always "meets" his guest too,† and even the comparatively casual English send to meet their guests.

A true host will of course take no compensation from his guest. He "feels hurt" by any offer to

---

* It is impolite to put them near the side post.

† "No hostess possessing the true spirit of hospitality will fail to meet her guests at the station or landing; or, if through any reason she cannot, a member of the family will be delegated to do so for her, she conducting them upon their arrival to their chambers, the host doing likewise for his male guests." (*The Complete Hostess*, p. 277.)

pay, having no intention of letting a guest cancel his debt in any such way.* When Dr. Felkin was in Uganda he went hungry at times, he tells us, because no M'ganda was allowed to sell anything to the King's visitors.[17] The "paying guest" is an entirely English innovation. In the United States even feeing the servants has to be done on the sly,† behind the back of one's host. Officially he knows nothing about it, and he is embarrassed if he catches his guest *in flagrante delicto*.

The least a host expects from an ex-guest is a return of hospitality. So well aware of this expectation are many persons that they will not accept hospitalities they cannot return. They know too well why they have been asked.

"Retayne a straunger after his estate and degree
Another tyme may happen he may doe as much for
    thee."[18]

More exacting hosts feel that they have been entertaining angels‡ unaware,—and angels al-

---

* Still apprehensive of the stranger, he may be afraid to take a gift from him, Westermarck suggests, gift-taking often involving a risk. (*The Origin and Development of the Moral Ideas*, i, 593.)

† Moreover a self-respecting servant will often refuse a fee, we are told, "especially if he or she be American born" [and so unwilling to recognise a class distinction?]. (*The Complete Hostess*, p. 286.)

‡ According to the *Hitopadesa*, "a guest consists of all the

ways express their gratitude in practical ways,—
or that hospitality is *per se* a means of acquiring
spiritual merit, magically or because of the religious sanction attaching to it. "The hospitable
reception of guests procures wealth, fame, long
life, and heavenly bliss," declares Manu,[19] the
famous Hindu code maker. Hospitality is indeed
a sacred duty.

The ceremonial character of hospitality is conspicuous at leave-taking in other particulars besides tipping. Set speeches are usually in order
between host and guest at that time. "*Kafikeni-
po*," "May you arrive safely," is said to the departing Wemba guest, a godspeed to which he makes
answer: "*Syaleni-po*," "May you remain here in
safety."[20] "*Maze kubalaba ngenze*," says a polite
M'ganda guest, "I have completed my visit and
am going." "*Kale genda*," answers his host, "All
right, you may go."[21] After tying up his things
the Masai guest says: "Well, I am about to go."
The owners of the kraal reply: "All right, good-
bye. Pray to God, accost only the things which
are safe, and meet nobody but blind people."
To this wish for a safe journey the guest responds:

---

deities." "Do not treat strangers slightingly," says the Ainu,
"for you never know whom you are entertaining." (Westermarck, *Moral Ideas*, i, 583.)

"Lie down with honey-wine and milk." "So be it," says the host, and then at last the guest is free to depart.[22] In the Andaman Islands the departing guest blows on his host's hand and says: "Here indeed I." His host answers: "Very well, go; when will you come again?" Guest: "I will bring away something for you one of these days." Host: "May no snake bite you!" Guest: "I will be watchful." Then each blowing on the hands of the other, they part, shouting invitations and promises for a future date until beyond earshot.[23] "Well, I must be going," says the departing American guest, declaring what a good time she has had and how grateful she feels. In return her hostess makes "some little civil speech" to show that she is sorry her guest must go so soon,[24] and that she hopes she will repeat her visit. She will underrate what she has done in the matter of hospitality, adding that at some future date she will indeed be able to do something for her guest. Then Maria will be home or the new wing will be finished or the strawberries will be ripe.

Other than verbal ceremonies are customary. A Persian accompanies his guest to the door, a ceremony called *mushaiyat*.[25] An American or English guest is apt to be solicited to write his name in a "guest book," a kind of pledge of him-

self, if one considers the magical connotation of
names. Greek host and guest broke a die, each
keeping a half as a souvenir. Quite often the
host makes his guest a gift at parting, gift-making
being a common way in primitive culture of ceremonially binding together two persons. "Because
he had sat on it," the Awemba sent Livingstone
the elephant's tusk which had served him in
court as a chair.[26] Desirous of paying his host a
compliment an Andaman Islander will ask to be
given one of the children of the family to bring up
as his own.[27] Among us, it is the guest rather
than the host who makes a gift—to the lady of the
house, "a new book, a deck of cards in a handsome case, a bit of handwork if you embroider,
some new music"; if you are a girl, flowers;
a "box of choice confections", if a man.*
"Though it be only a pincushion or a guard chain
of your own making,† it will have a certain value
as an expression of the gratitude which it becomes
you to feel."[28] To express his gratitude for the
hospitality he had received from the royal family

---

* *Dame Curtsey's Book of Etiquette*, p. 108. Chicago, 1910.
A man guest will often make a gift too on arrival, in this case
"the excellence or variety of the article only excusing the gift."
(*The Complete Hostess*, p. 285.)

† Obviously a gift made by oneself is more of a pledge. Hence
in the ceremonial of gift-making this feature is always emphasized. (See *The Complete Hostess*, p. 285.)

of Loango, on his return home a prince of Congo is said to have dedicated one of his wives to the tutelary god of his host.[29]   Unable to vie with an African potentate in graciousness,' the least an American guest can do, we are told, is to write host or hostess a "bread-and-butter letter." In fact not to do so would be extremely rude, a remissness not easily overlooked by a hostess. A hostess expects to receive this letter a day or two after her guest has reached home. The letter should "express in a few graceful words her thanks for the pleasure experienced and assure her hostess of her safe arrival."[30]   I transcribe the following "bread-and-butter" letter as sufficiently characteristic:

MY DEAR MRS. ——:

I shall not let another moment pass without telling you how much I enjoyed my visit to you, and how truly I appreciate all that you did to make my visit a delightful one. I shall keep in mind charming thoughts of the drives, walks, and happy days and evenings at Chestnut Hill.

Remember me most kindly to Mr. —— and believe me

Yours sincerely,

—— ——[31]

In circles where flexibility of expression if not of mind is more marked than at Chestnut Hill, the bread-and-butter letter admits, I am aware, of considerable variation. Not long ago I saw one written by a Harvard graduate who, like all the graduates of his period, had had the advantage of being brought up on "Alice." His letter was of one line and read: "It was the Best Butter."

Having surveyed the practice of hospitality along the lines of those who follow its rules and even of those who codify them, let us now define it from our general point of view. It appears to be a systematic attempt to overcome the suspicions and apprehensions always excited by the stranger. Its duties and obligations, its graces, together form a system for rendering him innocuous. He knows that as a guest it behooves him by his conformity and compliance to allay distrust or fear. A mannerly guest will be considerate of his host and lend himself to the devices taken to disarm him, devices sometimes of quarantine, sometimes of propitiation.

V

INTRODUCTIONS* AND DISINFECTANT RITES

A HOST is usually more or less responsible for his guest, whether he is his sponsor in the law courts as he was among the Romans, or takes his side in a quarrel as among the Akikúyu,[1] or as among us puts him up at the club or merely invites people to meet him at home. In England the mere presence of a guest is his guaranty. But in the United States, except in comparatively small circles, a guest requires an introduction. I have known persons sitting next to each other at a "dinner-party" unwilling to speak to each other until introduced by an acquaintance, one who had himself only been introduced perhaps before

* This subject I have considered important enough for a separate discussion, not only because of the example set me in this respect in all proper books on *les convenances,* but because the custom of introducing discovers the anxieties and timidities incident to enlarging one's circle of acquaintances as well as the precautions taken by society when it lets down barriers to raise up others. And I have been at the greater pains to particularize because many of the observances I mention are fast becoming obsolete.

44

going in to dinner. Sir Thomas Mitchell relates
that once in Australia on encountering a strange
native he asked his own native retainer to put a
question to him. But neither Blackfellow would
speak for awhile to the other. They stood apart,
neither looking at the other, and only after a
quarter of an hour or so would they enter into
conversation.[2] In the absence of an introduction
an awkward pause of this kind is in fact usual in
every primitive society. About to meet, certain
American Indian tribesmen would stop within
twenty yards or so of each other, writes one of
their observers, and sit or lie down for some minutes without speaking.[3] Except of necessity an
Ainu, it is said, is never the first to speak to a
stranger.[4] The other day the King of Spain was
precluded by native etiquette from speaking to an
ex-President of the United States who was travelling in the same train because the American had
not yet been presented at court by his ambassador.* Royalty is ever conservative.

An introduction is a short cut to conversation.

---

* In America the King might have been advised that "an acquaintance of either sex formed in travelling need never be retained
afterward, though sometimes valuable and valued friends are
thus secured." (Duffey, Mrs. E. B. *The Ladies and Gentlemen's
Etiquette: A Complete Manual of the Manners and Dress of American
Society*, p. 95. Philadelphia, 1887.)

It inspires confidence.* In more ways than one it is a voucher for the stranger. First there are the effects of naming. In primitive culture a man's name is an integral part of his personality. Knowledge of it, he believes, gives you power over him. Hence he often keeps his name a secret. In civilization too people sometimes refuse to be introduced, and in punctilious circles permission to make an introduction is usually sought.

Some name to go by one must have, however, and so a savage, no matter how secretive, finds it convenient to have a public as well as a secret name. Nor among us on making introductions is the Christian name or pet name or nickname used —even by an "old friend" or in certain circles by a member of the family. "There is nothing so awkward to a stranger as to be introduced to 'My brother Tom' or 'My sister Carrie.'"[5] I have heard mothers introduce their daughter as Miss So-and-So and in the United States husband and wife invariably introduce each other by their surname. Not to do so, it is felt, would be "undignified" or "lacking in respect," the terms we commonly use to express taboo.

---

*For we recall that "most friendships which have a legitimate beginning come through an acquaintanceship which opens by means of an introduction." (*Ib.*, p. 21.)

In several other particulars of good form in introducing the originally grave meaning of naming may be surmised. The order of naming, we may notice, is important. The less distinguished or the one to be less complimented is named first, the younger, the unmarried, the less notorious, the native, the man to the woman. Theirs must be the disadvantage, brief though it be, of having one's own name known to the other person without knowing his name or hers. But the disadvantage, it is generally felt, is not to be incurred unnecessarily. Told to speak the names of those he introduces "as low as possible . . . that all the world may not hear them,"[6] it sometimes happens that the introducer slurs over the name. He may feel that it is an awkward moment to be over with as quickly as possible—a sense of embarrassment of itself significant of the importance attached to introducing. Under these circumstances one of the two strangers is likely to say: "I beg your pardon, but I didn't catch your name."*

Although to forget a man's name is felt to create a very awkward situation, yet it is a common practice to open a conversation with, "You don't

---

*Or, "Pardon me, but I failed to hear your name." (*The Complete Hostess*, p. 320.)

remember my name." It is a challenge which undoubtedly puts the other person at a disadvantage, a disadvantage he is apt to admit and to attempt to overcome by answering, "Oh yes, I do," whether he recalls the name or not. His parry is feeble, for by a mere admission of forgetfulness would he not put his opponent to the disadvantage of having to tell his name? Telling your name is generally an "embarrassment," if not as among the Arabs a risk,* and most of us would sympathize with that Sir Frederick of Urbino who confessed to the assembled court that it troubled him to be asked who he was and what was his name.[7]

To directly ask a person his name is almost everywhere, we may notice, a rudeness, one seldom perpetrated except upon the very young.† But an introducer failing, the magnanimous or, among the Hindus, the respectful ‡ will volunteer their

*An Arab child is taught to conceal his family name from strangers lest he fall a victim to an intertribal blood feud. Nor does any Arab ever mention his family name to a stranger, whatever his tribe. (Burckhardt, p. 56.)

† Asking a child his age is one of the commonest ways in which an adult expresses his sense of superiority. A "natural" child will usually ignore the question.

‡ "A Brahmana who greets an elder must pronounce his name, saying, 'I am N. N.' . . . To his maternal and paternal uncles, fathers-in-law, officiating priests, and other venerable persons, he must say, 'I am N. N.' . . . even though they be younger

name, feeling it an essential preliminary to conversation. "My name is Smith," you graciously say; "Mine is Jones," says he. Without such an expression of mutual confidence, one of the two "chance acquaintances," particularly a lady, is quite liable to say in an emergency: "But I don't know you. I don't even know your name." Often after two persons have talked together without an introduction, and a mutual acquaintance arrives on the scene, an introduction is offered or even called for—a very striking instance of the significance attached to the ceremony. In closing a conversation in order to give it retrospectively a more satisfactory character, strangers will often tell each other their name, sometimes exchanging visiting-cards.*

than himself" [and apparently even though they already know his name quite well]. (*The Laws of Manu*, ii, 122, 130. *The Sacred Books of the East*, xxv.)

* Considerable importance attaches to the form of visiting-cards. With us they are invariably of white unglazed pasteboard engraved in black. "Plain script is never out of order, though other styles of engraving come and go." (*The Complete Hostess*, p. 306.) The fashionable size and shape vary, but a man's card is always smaller and narrower than a woman's. (*Ib.*, pp. 306, 309.) Chinese cards are printed in black on vermilion paper—except in mourning, when the paper is white with the name in blue. (Colquhoun, A. R. *Across Chrysê*, i, 19. London, 1883.) The formulas on Chinese visiting-cards are somewhat more ornate too than ours. They contain not only the name of the visitor but an address of respect to the host. For example, "The tender and sincere friend of your Lordship, and the perpetual

4

To many travellers a well-filled card-case is an indispensable part of their equipment.

Part of the idea in the exchange of visiting-cards by travellers may of course be utilitarian, based on a wish to continue an acquaintance.* There is too, in starting a conversation with a name, a practical feature. It may help to "place" a person. The edge is taken off a stranger, so to speak, if you know where he comes from or anything about his family or his own history. A Queensland Blackfellow who, away from home, does not tell the people he meets his name, who his father is, or where his mother comes from, is almost sure to be killed.[8] "What is your bird?" *i. e.* totem, is one of the first questions commonly put to a stranger by the Massim of New Guinea.[9] "What is the form of marriage of your people?" "Do you believe in anarchy?" "How old are

---

disciple of your doctrine, presents himself in this quality to pay his duty and make his reverence even to the earth." (Astley, iv, 80.)

* This can hardly be the reason for certain uses visiting-cards are put to, why, for example, Juliet's tomb at Verona is always filled with the visiting-cards of tourists, or why on the grave of a genius one sometimes sees a visiting-card, or why as we once drove through the streets of Tokyo as guests of the nation our carriages were filled with visiting-cards by the Japanese who packed the avenue to the railway-station. In such instances a visiting-card would seem to gratify a wish analogous to the wish to write your name in a notorious place, a wish, I take it, like the wishes prompting other forms of introduction, of participation.

you?" are questions put to the stranger at the ports of the United States. Obviously, once classified, once related to familiar facts, the stranger anywhere is less unfamiliar and alarming. An introduction is soothing, tranquillizing. Even a public assemblage likes to have introduced to it its speakers, and a public speaker himself is quite willing to submit to the slight embarrassment of being introduced, knowing the easing and thereby disarming effect of it upon his audience.*

But the chief immunity-giving character of an introduction lies in the introducer himself. He vouches for the man he introduces. His sense of responsibility varies of course and the degree to which he is held responsible. As a rule he cannot be too careful. He has a number of rules to guide him. He must not introduce a gentleman to a lady without first asking her permission, a permission not to be refused, however, without "very good and strong reasons."[10] A gentleman does not introduce one lady to another and even a lady should be careful about introducing two women living in the same place.[11] Gentlemen

---

*The presiding officer who is called upon to introduce a celebrity is also aware of the propitiatory nature of the introduction. Feeling that it is indispensable, but at the same time struck by the superficial absurdity of it, he compromises with some such formula as, "I don't need to introduce to you, etc."

do not ask for an introduction to each other, nor should they be introduced to each other at a club, in the street, or, some think, even in a drawing-room. Is this rule held to because, as one writer on etiquette says, "gentlemen do not generally wish to become acquainted,"[12] or because less timorous than the ladies they do not feel the need of protecting themselves with an introduction?*

There are certain times and places too where one is cautioned not to be hasty in introducing—at the theatre, for example, in travelling, in the street. "If one gentleman joined me in the street while I was walking with another, I should certainly *not* introduce the former to the latter," writes the author of *Social Customs*,[13] "because," she adds, "he would have no business to join me unless he knew the gentleman with whom I was walking."† Introductions made on the street, under ordinary circumstances at least, are not at any rate consequential. None needs to "be bound by a casual introduction of this sort given as a matter of form, and where no real acquaintance‡ has been made between the parties."[14]

* Such would appear to be the view of another writer on etiquette who says that men "are supposed to be at liberty to speak to each other in society without formal presentation." (Learned, p. 96.)

† Is this taboo a trifling by-product of male proprietorship?

‡ From the point of view of making an acquaintance a ball-

Introductions may, as we know, be written. Perhaps because of the impressiveness characteristic of writing, a written introduction is more weighty than an oral introduction and its author incurs greater responsibility. "It is rash to give letters unless to people whom one knows well,* or at least knows all about."[15] Of course one cannot set forth all this knowledge in the letter of introduction—if for no other reason than that it is left unsealed or should be; but as in the oral introduction, some clue to the person introduced should be given. Passports† or international letters of introduction give such information in considerable detail, even to the colour of the eyes.

Public or private letters of introduction and their precursors before the art of writing, rings, seals, scarfs, message sticks, etc., imply a common acquaintance. Under circumstances where common acquaintances are not available, where there is none to assume responsibility for the

room seems to be classified, at times, with a street. "In England an introduction given for dancing purposes does not constitute acquaintanceship." (Ward, p. 218.) But there appear to be circles in this country too where "a ball-room acquaintance does not extend beyond the evening in which it is formed." (Duffey, p. 79.)

* "It is especially rash to give letters to foreigners," adds our authority.

† "Body-protecting charms" they were once called in China. (Colquhoun, *Across Chrysê*, i, 95.)

stranger, there is nothing to do but disinfect him
—once you decide to admit him—or to admit him
with precautions.   A Victorian tribe approaching
another unknown to it carry burning sticks to
purify, they say, the air.[16] When Captain Moresby
landed on New Guinea, a medicine-man exorcised
the evil spirit in him by magical jugglery with
palm leaves and by playing a kind of leapfrog.[17]
At Ushuri, one of the villages of the Soudan, when
visitors are at the gate they are asked to step
over a live fowl held over the threshold.   The
fowl is then killed, and all "to bring good luck."[18]
In Benin the feet of strangers were ceremonially
washed,* and sentinels at the gates of Yoruba
towns often oblige European travellers to wait till
nightfall before admitting them, fearing that in
the daytime the devil would tag on behind them.[19]
The descendants of the Yorubans in Hayti, I
once learned to my cost, allow no strange craft
to cast anchor in their harbours after sundown.

---

*Frazer, p. 108.   Frazer seems to hold that the stranger is
disliked because he is suspected of magic.   Is he not rather
suspected of magic because he is disliked?   You dislike him
because he discomfits you and so you "spot" magic, magic, if
you are a savage, being your usual explanation of discomfiture.

VI

CASTE

WITH the utmost precaution introductions are not always in order. You do not introduce your butler to your guest, nor are shop girls presented at the court of St. James. Royalty is at any rate apt to be confined to a limited circle of acquaintances. The Emperor of China seldom left his palace. When he did go out, none looked at him*; even the guards who lined his route turned their backs. The Kings of Corea did not leave their palaces at all. The King of Fernando Po lives in a crater into which no White Man may ever descend. The ruler of the Baduwis of Java never quits his capital and subjects who live outside of it may not see him.[1] People from all over the United States may at stated times enter the

---

* A cat may not everywhere look at a king, nor does a person of position always look at a person of none. I was once a party to a practical joke, the point of which was to see whether a certain lady would recognize her own son were he to attend us, her guests, as a valet. She did not, as she never looked at his face.

White House to see the President and even shake
hands with him, but it would be impossible for a
President to live in Washington outside of the
White House, no President has ever left the
country during his term of office,* and many
Americans consider it "undignified" for a President to travel much even within its boundaries.

Even when royalties are more migratory, they
do not mix much with the world. To see the
King of Dahomi or the Muata Jamwo of the
Congo at their meals is a capital offence. When
the King of Cazembe raised his glass to drink
or when the King of Tonga ate, all present pro-
strated themselves, looking away, or all turned
their backs.² The King of the Awemba has
probably always to eat at home for only flour
prepared by his wives may be served to him.³
In Washington the President of the United States
dines out openly only with the members of his
cabinet. He is free, however, to invite people—
all kinds of people saving negroes and anarchists
—to dine with him at the White House.

When the King of Persia gave dinner parties
he himself sat at a separate table in a separate

---

* Were he to cross the boundary, I suspect the outcry would
equal that of Islam when Sultan Abdul Aziz made his unprece-
dented visits to Queen Victoria, Napoleon III, and the Emperor
of Austria.

room where he could see his guests, unseen by them. [4] Many another ruler has had to eat entirely in private without the sight of a guest or even a wife for company. In other particulars the ways of royalty may also have to be screened from the public. At several courts it does not do for the sovereign merely to raise his hand to his mouth when he sneezes, a cloth has to be held up by a courtier in front of his face. Not only when he sneezed but when he coughed, spat, or took snuff, a cloth was similarly held up before the face of the King of Jebu, a Slave Coast king. The Sultan of Wadai always speaks from behind a curtain. [5] Graham Bell has told me that in an audience he once had with Queen Victoria to tell her about the new telephone, she asked him questions through a third person, keeping him at a distance quite as effectually as if she were talking over his telephone.* When King Mutesa was being physically examined by Dr. Felkin, all the courtiers in attendance had to turn away, [6] and it is customary in Uganda to call a King's illness, whatever it may be, *senyiga*, a severe cold [7]—a device not unparalleled in European courts. In

---

* The rulers of Uganda and Dahomi also communicated through a third person. (Spencer, Herbert. *The Principles of Sociology*, ii, 28–9. New York, 1900.)

the court of Edward IV even the Queen's laun-
dresses had "to bee sworne to keepe the chambre
counsaylle."[8]

The seclusive habits of royalty are peculiarly
conspicuous, but throughout society there are many
other seclusive or exclusive groups. Imitation
being the truest flattery as well as an instinct,
court circles are naturally exclusive. The courtier
of Urbino is advised "not to renn, wrastle, leape,
nor cast the stone or barr with men of the Coun-
trey, except to be sure to gete the victorie—for it is
to ill a sight and to foule a matter and without estimation to see a Gentilman overcome by
a Cartar and especially in wrastling." Even
"dancing in the Sun" with the country people
is open to the question at the court of Urbino of
"what a man shal gaine by it."[9] I once heard
one of our ambassadors to Berlin sharply criticized
because his wife not only did her own marketing
but went to market on a bicycle; and a Washington
observer has lately told us that the present Secre-
tary of the Interior is being criticized for riding
on trolley cars and standing on the rear platform
at that—"that doesn't *go* in Washington."

Familiarities between persons of different social
position are discountenanced elsewhere. "Fancy
the moral condition of that society in which a

lady of fashion joked with a footman," exclaimed
Thackeray, horror struck by the ways of his people
in the days of Queen Anne. No Ashantee of con-
sequence drinks before his inferiors without hiding
his face from them.* A New Zealand slave does
not eat of his master's food nor cook at the same
fire.[10]

"Vche Exstate syngulerly in halle shalle sit adowne
That none of hem se othure at mete tyme in feld nor
in town."[11]

And the English upper servant still refuses to
eat with the other servants. There are houses
too in New England where the choreman is no
longer expected to eat with the family. Nor may
inferiors and superiors in the Tonga Islands eat
together.[12] Most Hindus would not eat with
persons of another caste. Many other caste
separations occur in India. A Puliah has to keep
a distance of one hundred paces away from persons of other castes. A Pariah may put only one
foot inside the house of his master, and through
a village street lived in by Brahmans he may not
even pass. Nor, firmly believing that it would
lead to ruin, will he let a Brahman pass through
his own quarter.[13] No labourer in his working

* Were he to drink more publicly, would he be charged, I
wonder, with playing to the gallery?

clothes would walk down Fifth Avenue with a
"lady." "I'd like to show you the town," said
my Wyoming driver to me an afternoon I spent
in Cody, "though I'm not used to walking with
a lady."*

"I won't get drunk anyhow," he added. And
as we walked down the street where acquaintances
grinned at him from the door of every saloon, I
appreciated the assurance. Being a gentleman,
whatever he called himself, it was natural for him
to wish to reassure me, once he had put me into a
caste not his own. Apprehensiveness, he was well
aware, is felt by a member of one caste concerning
a member of another. An English booby "is
frightened out of his wits when people of fashion
speak to him," writes Lord Chesterfield.[14] Contact with royalty or with royal things is often
accounted dangerous. The Nubas of East
Africa believed they would die if they entered
the house of their priestly king or sat on the
stone he used for a seat. A Cazemba of Angola
believes that he who touches the King dies unless

---

* Nevertheless, fortunately for me, it had not occurred to him
that civilities "ought not to be extended to persons who belong
to either a higher or a lower class of society." The former, adds
Mrs. Ward, are "warranted in looking upon you as pushing; the
latter are apt to consider you as patronizing." (*Sensible Etiquette*, p. 394. Philadelphia, 1878.)

liar ways. Once realized, whatever their origins, caste characteristics tend to become arbitrary or compulsory. Rarely does anyone want his caste habits interfered with or imitated. Rarely does anyone want to interfere with or imitate the caste habits of others. Each caste wants its members to conform to its regulations and the members of other castes to conform to theirs. Hence caste distinctions are enforced by taboos or laws, by an endless miscellany of restrictions. For example, kings, unlike commoners, may not go a-courting. Sometimes they are not allowed to marry at all. Sometimes they may marry only women with peculiar characteristics or of a given lineage. In Aracan, India, for the girls selected every year as the most eligible for the King's harem, odour was the criterion. [17] In ancient Egypt and in the Peru of the Incas the rulers had to marry their own sisters. Once the King of Loango is crowned, the one wife allowed him must be a Cabinda princess. [18] Recently the British government jailed a man for saying that the King had made an ordinary marriage. More recently a German princess is said to have killed herself because she was not allowed to make one. In other particulars, too, royal habits are strictly regulated. A king may be limited in his choice of colour. The Sumatran

Sultan of Menancabow had constantly to wear yellow.[19] Black may not be worn ordinarily in the court of Japan. Kukulu, a divine king in West Africa, was never allowed to lie down.* Among the Ewes the king neither ate nor slept,[20] at least it was criminal not to think so. Mutesa of Uganda never smoked, although outside of the court every man and woman in his country was a steady smoker.[21] The President of the United States is allowed to smoke, but I doubt if smoking would be tolerated in his wife, for she—and he too in other respects—is expected to set an example to the people, an expectation that must entail, if lived up to, a number of peculiar habits.†

Of sumptuary law or custom we may cite a few instances. Among the Sioux only medicine-men

---

* Lest he should thereby cause the wind to drop unduly. (Bastian, A., *Die Deutsche Expedition an der Loango-Küste*, i, 288. Jena, 1874.)

† Whether royalties are held responsible for the blowing of the winds or for the morals of their people, royal taboos are obviously onerous. No wonder that rulers have sometimes abdicated or that thrones sometimes stand vacant. Bastian found at the time of his visit to Angoy that the throne had been vacant ten years, so exacting were the Angoy taboos on royalty. (*Expedition an der Loango-Küste*, i, 368.) In the United States there are already many high offices difficult to fill and some day the highest of them may go begging, the task of being the public preceptor *par excellence* having become intolerably burdensome. Even to-day representing the President abroad entails obligations many men have been unwilling to assume.

may wear a necklace of bear's claws whenever they like.[22] For a time in Uganda nobody outside of the royal family was allowed to wear European cloth.[23] In Corea the lower classes may wear neither silk nor purple.[24] Under Philip Augustus the length of French shoe points was determined by social position, ranging from six to twelve inches. In the sixteenth century French women were jailed by scores for wearing clothes like those of their superiors.[25] "Even in a Republican country like our own," once wrote an American woman, "I conceive it would be impracticable and impolitic . . . to abolish entirely* . . . the distinctions . . . in the different classes of society in respect to dress."[26] In the United States and in Uganda the upper classes and only the upper classes carry a walking-stick.[27] The origin of it in Uganda I do not know; with us we always hear that it is a relic of the day when a gentleman and only a gentleman carried a sword. To-day

* Since this was written they have been abolished—in theory. And yet perhaps the older theory does float about in some back waters. "Your cook wouldn't wear that dress," you may be told by a senior in your family when you are dressed worse than usual. The maid who dresses like her mistress is still a source of humour on the stage. An editorial in *The Times* of June 10, 1914, ridicules a workman who had testified that his wages were not ample to dress on. "What next!" exclaims the editor. "Won't he be wanting to wear evening clothes to the play?"

in Uganda only gentlemen are allowed to carry copper spears.

Uganda gentlemen when they meet offer each other coffee berries—instead of cigarettes. The offer of either is a habit peculiar to the gentleman. In the United States cigarette smoking by women is a habit even more confined to the upper class. Only "society ladies" are supposed to smoke.* A Brahman who drinks arrack loses caste.[28] In Fiji the common people were not allowed to eat human flesh, nor in San Salvador to drink chocolate.[29] With us the servant who drinks his master's champagne or eats his game not only wastes his master's substance, but outrages his sense of caste propriety.

Games as well as weapons, narcotics, or foods are apt to be a caste taboo or, according to your point of view, a caste monopoly. In England in the sixteenth century playing "at the Tables, Tennis, Dice, Cards, Bowls, Clash, Coyting, Logating" were forbidden, on penalty of a fine of twenty shillings, to artisans, husbandmen, labourers, servants, sailors, or fishermen, except at Christmas, and even at Christmas none was to play in his master's house or presence.[30] Are

---

*In many respects indeed the manners of these ladies are said to be quite different from those not "in society."

5

there not to-day Anglo-Saxon masters or at least mistresses who would feel outraged or at least annoyed to see their servants playing on the tennis court or on the drawing-room piano? At any rate they would not think of playing duets with them or challenging them to a set of tennis. Not so unscrupulously would they offend against the old maxim:

"Pley thou not but with thy peres."[31]

Occupations are everywhere an affair of caste restrictions. The Wahuma are the recognized herdsmen of Uganda, and it would be even more difficult to induce a Uganda tribesman to tend cattle[32] than in the United States to get a white man to become a parlour-car porter or the native-born to work with the "Dago" in the ditch. In India the great fourfold division of Hindu society is based on occupation, on the business of being a priest or a king, a householder or a menial, and within these main divisions there is an endless number of sub-castes characterized by occupation —fishermen, basket weavers, dancers, blacksmiths, etc. Manual labour or labour of any kind is in many places a caste privilege. The *Niang-pan*, the two classes of nobility of Corea, the civil and military, would not dream of working, nor would it

be allowed them. [33]   There was a time in England
when a lord might have found it impossible to get a
job as a cashier, let us say, or a stoker, and there
are business houses in this country averse to employing youths who have been through college
or whose fathers are rich men.   As for the daughters of the rich or of any claimant of social position, they are generally told that they owe it to
their family not to go to work.   "People would
say I can't afford to support you," exclaims an
indignant and remonstrant parent.   Outside of the
family the young woman is told she ought not take
the bread out of the mouth of girls having to earn
their living.

The "advantages" of education are very commonly a caste monopoly.   In Greece it was forbidden to teach the art of painting to servants
and slaves.   A statute of Richard II decreed that
no child who had laboured in husbandry until
twelve should be "put to any Mystery or Handi-
craft," nor, according to a statute of Henry IV,
should the son or daughter of any person whose income was not at the least twenty shillings a year. [34]
Modern trade unions set a limit to the number of
their apprentices.   As late as the middle of the
nineteenth century in one English village the squire
would allow only reading to be taught in school; in

another village arithmetic was taboo—"the boys
would be getting to know too much about wages."[35]
The schooling of peasants is discouraged in Russia.
It was at one time illegal in our South to teach
negroes to read and write. To teach the "working
classes" anything but the three R's is sure to make
them dissatisfied, we are told by critics of the
curriculum of the public schools. "It only unfits
them for their station in life." The privilege of a
college education is still more or less dependent
upon the parental income, and quite properly so,
said to me only last year a president of one of our
great universities.

Caste is observed in the proprieties of address
and of language. Before addressing his king a
Wemba lies on his back and claps his hands.[36]
A Fiji Islander crouches down, rubbing the upper
part of the left arm with the right hand.[37] In
Washington none may sit while the President
stands. Throughout the country gentlemen nod
to quite a number of classes who take their hats off
in return. A gentleman will nod too to persons he
passes on the road if they do not look like gentlemen. With one another the gentry have to be
more formal—a bow would not necessarily be an
act of condescension. It might indeed be a piece
of presumption. "It is not the correct thing to

bow first to a person of higher social position and exclusive views, where only a slight acquaintance exists." [38]

In Fiji all references to the person of a chief or to his acts are sufficiently hyperbolized to constitute a chiefly dialect. [39] In Samoa there are many terms not to be used in the presence of a chief, at least without the apologetic phrase *vaeane*, "saving your presence." There are, for example, "polite" terms for "come," "sit," "eat," "die," "sick," "anger," "sleep," "the chief's house." [40] Then, too, in Samoa and elsewhere, if the name of any object is taken by the chief as his own, the object has to be renamed,* no matter how common a word its name may be.† Every caste in Japan has its own peculiar "I," a pronoun no other caste may use. [41] Formerly in Germany every superior was addressed indirectly as *er*, "he," just as to-day

---

* Analogous renaming occurs in connection with the dead. This taboo, and the still more common taboo on their own name are, I believe, barriers against them. If such name taboos were but tokens of "respect," why would it be the outrage it is usually held to be, or at any rate the lack of tact, for the outsider to mention the name of the deceased?

† Obviously it is easy enough for an inconsiderate chief to upset the language. We may deem ourselves fortunate that our President is more restricted in introducing verbal novelties and is even criticized for expressing ideas on modified spelling. Our use of titles of respect—Mister, Captain, Doctor, etc.—is a more comfortable caste provision too than grammatical differentiations.

to be polite the Italian addresses you in the third person feminine.   Among Anglo-Saxons it is still considered good form to refer to yourself in writing to inferiors in the third person—unless you are a king or a newspaper editor, when the first person plural is proper.   Among the Abipones of the upper class the names of men end in *in*, the names of women in *en*, and these syllables you must add to nouns and verbs in talking to them.[42]   The Abipone nobles moreover use words quite peculiar to their own caste.[43]   The vocabulary of our own upper classes is materially different from that of our lower, and many words or phrases are taboo as unbecoming a lady or a gentleman.   No person of any social pretensions can afford to talk like a fishwife or a groom.   Billingsgate and Cockneyisms are not tolerated.   To speak correct English is a passport into good society.   To be treated like a gentleman one must talk like one—even to the forgoing of puns according to certain authorities,* or of proverbs according to Lord Chesterfield. If "you should let off a proverb, and say, That what is one man's meat is another man's poison; or else, Everyone as they like, as the good man said

---

* A gentleman never condescends to be a punster, says Mrs. Abell. (*Woman in her Various Relations*, p. 121.   New York, 1853.   Cp. Hall, p. 244.)

when he kissed his cow,—everybody would be persuaded that you had never kept company with anybody above footmen and housemaids,"[44]— unless you lived in Fiji or on the West Coast of Africa or in many another tribal society where proverbs and adages seem to be in vogue even among the "smartest" people.

At these caste differences of speech, as in fact at all the other caste differences I have mentioned, we have taken but the most cursory glance. The history of caste is unwritten; analysis of political, economic, and cultural classes is extremely scant, even description of them as they exist in given groups is fragmentary or wholly lacking. In this discussion therefore I could but present illustrations of some types of caste barriers and of certain caste peculiarities which must serve of themselves as interclass barriers, and of the existence in certain cases of interclass fear, inferring that a relation of cause and effect exists between caste barrier and caste fear, the barrier being raised because of fear, and once raised becoming the source of further apprehension.

VII

A POSTSCRIPT ON CHIVALRY

AFTER an afternoon spent dancing in a popular
cabaret a certain lady of high society, the
story comes to us from Paris, looking at her watch
remarked hastily that she must hurry off. She
had an early dinner. "I too must be going, Madame, I too have an early dinner," rejoined her
accomplished partner. And lo, that evening at
dinner Madame perceived that her new acquaintance was as accomplished in serving a dinner as
in dancing the tango. In Cody, Wyoming, our
ways were still more "democratic." We danced
of an evening with our chambermaid quite well
aware of her rôle by day, and after complimenting
our cook upon one of his dishes, we engaged in an
argument with him which was settled only by an
appeal to the dictionary. Here in New York,
however, there is less of such fraternity than in
Cody or in Paris. Your Continental cook would be
amazed if you asked her the meaning of any word

off the menu and she would undoubtedly be greatly embarrassed if you even asked her to eat with you. Like Sancho Panza under similar circumstances she would probably decline your invitation.* Nor would she like you to give up your seat to her in the street car. You do, of course, if you are truly chivalrous.†

In chivalry more emphasis has ever been placed upon the inferiority of sex than upon the inferiority of caste. Knighthood was a caste like any other, with many of the typical caste marks, a matter of birth, education, initiation, equipment. But in chivalry, its code, it made a new psychological contribution to caste distinctions, one endowing it with unusual endurance. Borrowing from Christianity, chivalry emphasized the subjective sense of superiority at the expense of the objective. Whatever outward marks of caste a knight, or a gentleman to use the more modern term, has had

* "Gramercy for your favour!" cried Sancho; "but I may tell your worship that, provided I had plenty to eat, I could eat it as well, and better, standing, and by myself, than if I were seated on a level with an Emperor; and, indeed, if I must speak the truth, I relish much more what I eat in my corner without niceties or ceremonies." (*Don Quixote*, pt. i, ch. xi.) "Kutte nouhte youre mete eke as it were Felde men" (Furnivall, p. 7. About 1475), or, as we say, "don't eat like a boor." Table manners are, I suppose, one of our most marked class distinctions.

† In the privacy of home you may be more willing to consider her prejudices.

to forego, thanks to political revolution * or *bour-geois* or plutocratic invasion, in his heart he is always a gentleman. Nor can any vicissitude of fortune ever keep a lady from being a lady. However she is dressed, you can always "tell" a lady†; whatever his company, a gentleman.

Whatever his company, too, at home in it a gentleman is bound to be. "A real well-bred man would speak to all the kings in the world with as little concern and as much ease as he would speak to you,"[1] writes a great gentleman. But Lord Chesterfield was far from implying that a gentle-

---

* A democracy like the United States is the very stronghold of chivalry. Where else is there as much talk of being a "thorough gentleman" or a "perfect lady" or of acting like a gentleman or a lady, and where else is the charge of being "common" or a *parvenu* or a *nouveau riche* so much resented? Does not some of the intolerance bestowed in certain Eastern circles upon the vulgarities of the plutocrat betray dislike of the idea that wealth can overcome caste barriers? And does not the American cherish chivalry because it gives him a sense of superiority and leaves him innocent of any sense of being undemocratic?

† An expertness in which we are superior to the Kakhyen. All the tribesmen looking the same, half-naked, unkempt, and grimy, they have to ascertain verbally each other's class. So the first question one Kakhyen puts to another is: "Are you a noble or a commoner?" (Parker, E. H., "The Burmo-Chinese Frontier and the Kakhyen Tribes." *Fortnightly Review*, p. 94, July, 1897.) Now with us a lady, no matter how shabbily or how scantily attired, wears her clothes, one always hears, "like a lady." Lately to be sure she has been reproached by certain newspaper editors for dressing like a *demi-mondaine*, inconsiderately denying her caste.

man's manners should always be the same. "For my own part, I am more upon my guard as to my behaviour to my servants and others who are called my inferiors, than I am towards my equals." Undoubtedly the noble lord never argued with them or lost his temper. He believed in having two sets of manners. So did some centuries before him one Hugh Rhodes of the King's Chapel.

"If thou play, game, or sporte, with thy inferyour by byrth,
    Use gentle pastyme, men will then commend you in your myrth."[2]

Evidently the prejudice against having more than one set of manners is fairly modern. Is it the outcome of an homogeneity-exacting democracy or is it the last refinement of arrogance on the part of the gentry, their final assertion of caste? For, if, thanks to his inner sense of superiority, a gentleman may be at ease with royalty, he is even more likely to feel secure with his acknowledged inferiors and to forgo many outward measures of defence, even the barrier of a special set of manners.*

* The barrier of "manners" is neatly touched off by Mrs. Abell. If an acquaintance "is found to be undesirable an increased observance of ceremony is the most delicate way of showing it, and a person would be very obtuse who would not take such a hint." (*Woman in Her Various Relations*, p. 140.)

"The best manner is no manner" is a favourite saying of a gentleman of my acquaintance, and a very fine gentleman he is.

Chivalry has been based indeed on the feeling that because the stranger, women, children, the old, the "inferior" from status or personal weakness, could not encroach upon you, you might dispense with some of the usual barriers against them quite safely. The very protection you afford them is a barrier in itself against them. It keeps them most rigorously and most subtly in their place. Since the place given them is exalted, it is plainly ungrateful and unreasonable in them to wish to leave it. Stay in it they must, if they are to get the benefits offered them. If ever they show any signs of leaving it, they not only risk losing their advantages, but they act inconsiderately towards their protectors. As soon as there is any self-assertion, no matter how unconvincing, by the "weaker," the "stronger" becomes demoralized, panic-struck. The one barrier he has counted on is threatened, he realizes, and threatened in the only way he fears—by implications of its superfluity. The merest hint that chivalry is not needed causes chivalry to fall to pieces, prompting the sometime chivalrous to resort to older and cruder means of self-defence, to insistence upon the prerogatives of seniority or upon privileges of caste other than chivalrous or up-on sex exclusiveness in forms more direct and more substantial.

VIII

ACQUAINTANCES

A N introduction once over and assurances given,* an attempt to "place" an acquaintance is generally made. His name, we noted, may be a help. A "tactful" introducer is still more helpful. She will mention the place the nominee comes from—Mr. C. of Washington let us say—or she will make some remark to start conversation, such as, "Mr. C. has just returned from a trip to Colorado"[1] or "recently returned from Europe."† If Mr. C. is a celebrity, that fact, we are told, should also be brought out. For example: Mr. C. "the artist, whose pictures you have frequently

---

* "I am much pleased, I am much rejoiced," says the Snake Indian. (Spencer, ii, 151.) "I am glad to meet you," or "I am happy to make your acquaintance," we usually say. At any rate some remark should be made at once. (Learned, p. 94.)

† In the Soudan travellers do not have to depend upon the form of their introduction—or upon the hotel labels on their valises—to show they have been abroad. After they have been down to the coast the Wanyamwezi of the interior change their names. (Wilson and Felkin, i, 43.)

seen," or Mr. C., "author of *The World After the
Deluge*, which you so greatly admired."[2]

Mutual acquaintances, attendance at the same
school or church, the opera or the circus, any celebration attracting public attention,* are other conversational openings. Common experiences in the
professions or in trade, in child-bearing, in house-
keeping, as tourists† are also favourite topics
of conversation, reassuring aids past the perils of
first acquaintance.‡ For common experiences of
this kind imply common reactions, *i. e.* that your
new acquaintance is like yourself, hence "a safe
acquaintance."

Herein lies the social value of slang, of proverbs
and aphorisms, of "funny stories," of commonplaces, and of catchwords. All are pledges, so to
speak, that your companion thinks and feels as
you do—if you are a "sociable" man. In other

---

*For example in New Guinea the *Barlum* or great initiation
ceremony. When it is on it is said the men talk of nothing else.
(Webster, Hutton. *Primitive Secret Societies*, p. 31. New York,
1908.)

† But you are advised, if you wish to please, not to boast of
your travels (Ward, p. 392), travelling, we recall, being an asset.

‡ But even with "old" acquaintances you are advised "if you
really wish to be thought . . . amiable and unselfish" to lead the
way "for sportsmen to talk of their shooting, a mother to talk
of her children, a traveller of his journeys and the countries he has
seen, a young lady of her last ball and the prospective ones, an
artist of his picture, and an author of any book that he has
written." (*Ib.*, p. 401.)

words, belonging to the same group, you and he
have the same ways. You are likely to find each
other companionable. In speech at least you are
unlikely to disconcert each other since you make
no personal demand on each other. Proverbs and
aphorisms require no response. Rather they check
response, closing the subject. The only way to
meet an aphorism is with another. Similarly a
funny story prompts a return in kind. The laughter it evokes implies a group point of view, a
common sense of humour.* Even more than
funny stories commonplaces imply a group point
of view, calling for merely an impersonal, tradi-
tional response.

Of a like social value are familiar forms or formulas of salutation, of polite enquiry or concern, of
farewell, of congratulation or condolence, in short
of all "expressions of sympathy."

"Passing the time of day" is in many places an
acceptable formula of greeting, safely impersonal.
"You have come with the dew on you," says one
Samoan to another in the early morning, changing
later to, "You have come in the heat of the sun,"

---

*The experienced orator is apt to open with a "good story";
he knows how reassuring it is to his audience. To meet fully the
demand for this particular kind of satisfaction, communities may
produce a special functionary, the court jester or the professional
humourist.

"You have come in the darkness."[3] "May your day be white," says one Arab in Cairo to another. "May yours be like milk," his acquaintance has to rejoin.[4] "Good day," say we, "the top of the morning to you," "*bon soir*," "*gute nacht*," and often we go on to talk about the weather in more detail, and even less personally than with a good wish implicit. A good wish in a greeting may extend over the day. The Brahman who has been polite enough to tell his name* should be saluted in return with: "Mayst thou be long-lived,† O gentle one!"[5]

It is important for salutations in particular to be reassuring. "It is well," was the salutation of the Hebrews, and the Shunamite woman gives it even when she is about to announce the death of her son.[6] "All is well," says the messenger to David, regardless of the death of Absalom.[7] But even under less trying circumstances salutations should inspire confidence. Besides it is always possible that your acquaintance has changed since you

---

* See p. 48.

† "And the word 'a' must be added at the end of the name, the syllable preceding it being drawn out the length of three moras"— no trifle was a salutation to the high-caste Hindu. "To those persons who, when a name is pronounced, do not understand the meaning of the salutation a wise man should say, 'It is I'; and he should address in the same manner all women." (*Manu*, ii, 123.)

last met, making all the more imperative some familiarity upon meeting. "You haven't changed a bit," "You are as young as ever," "You are just the same as when we last met," are some of the compliments* we pay after an absence. Merely noticing the separation has a good effect. "*La nauichi?*" "Now are you come?" says the Abipone.[8] "You have come quickly," says the Japanese regardless of the time the coming has really taken.[9] Almost as regardless we say, "You have been long in coming" or "I haven't seen you for such a long time" or "It is an age since we met." The awkwardness of meeting may also be lessened by saying: "What *have* you been doing with yourself?" "Have you been working hard?" may be said to a man; to a girl, "I suppose you have been having a gay time." Even when the need of noticing an absence or in some cases of ignoring it† is not felt, a salutation should not be abrupt or startling. Better even than a question about what the other has been doing is a reference to what he is engaged upon. "*Sa yadra*," "You are awake," says one Fijian early in the day to another.[10] "*Ua mapu mai*," "You are rested," is the civil Samoan salutation to a man

---

* Let us note the implication in these compliments that any change is to the bad.   † See p. 150.

returning from fishing; "*Ua matu*," "You are dry," or "*Faemalū*," "You are cool," to one who has just had his bath.[11] Among the Pueblo Indians I have noticed similar amenities. A man stops to speak to a woman laundering her clothes in the creek. "You are washing," he says, just as we in passing a man with a gun would say, "You are going hunting," or a girl sitting under a tree with a book, "You are reading."

The form of salutation is necessarily stable, but in different groups it varies considerably. Baring the shoulder on the Gold Coast, as Burton points out, is like unhatting in England.[12] In New Ireland when one man says to another, "I am glad to see you," he pats him on the head[13]; with us he slaps his shoulder. In continental Europe the slap is rather an embrace, and men as well as women kiss. The Samoan or Fijian kiss is a sniff[14]; the Burmese, a sniff with a pressure of lips and nose to cheek.[15] To greet another the Balonda claps his hands and digs himself in the ribs[16]; the Ainu rubs the palms of his hands together and strokes his beard.[17] There are several variations in handshaking. In the Banks Islands a man locks the middle finger of his right hand with his friend's fingers and then pulls it away with a crack,[18] a manœuvre, I have been told, something like the greeting between members of our Greek letter secret societies. A M'kikúyu spits on his hand before giving it to you to shake.[19] The handshake of the Arab seems to be a scuffle in which each tries to raise to his lips the hand of the other.*

While the Arab is shaking your hand or, like the Chinaman, kissing his own hand for you, he repeats, "How art thou?"†—an inquiry he may renew several times if he is well-bred, during the course of your conversation.[20] The inquiry about your health or condition in general,—"How do you do?" "*Comment vous portez-vous?*" "*Mwapoleni?*" "Are your wounds healed?"‡ "How do you perspire?"§ "How have the mosquitoes used you?"‖ —is extended to inquiry about your family, *their* health, occupations, whereabouts, particularly their whereabouts. "*Otyano?*" "How are you?" asks the M'ganda, taking your right hand, or if he likes you and has not seen you for some time, putting his head on your shoulder. "*Ah, ah, otyano?*" "No, no [*i.e.* there is nothing wrong]; how are you?" you answer. "*Ah*," says the other. "*Ah*," you say.

---

* Herein Herbert Spencer sees the origin of our own handshaking. (*The Principles of Sociology*, ii, 139.)
† "*Allek toy*," "I hope you are well," says the Bedouin. (Burckhardt, p. 107.)
‡ Wemba. (Gouldsburg and Sheane, p. 256.)
§ Cairo. (Mallery, p. 208.)   ‖ Orinoco. (*Ib.*, p. 209.)

And so you keep it up until one says *"Agafayo?"*
"How is it where you come from?" *"Nungi,"*
"Well." *"Agafayo?"* "How is it where you come
from?" *"Nungi. Atewamwe batya?"* "Well.
How are your relations?"[21] An American, and
married, you are asked about your husband or
wife: "Where is John?" "What's he doing now?"
"Is Maria here?" "Is she better than she was?"
A parent, you are unfailingly asked about the
children just as the children, as they grow older,
will be asked about you. "I suppose you don't see
much of him, now he is away in school?" "Isn't
it nice to have her with you?" With us, as among
the Ainu,[22] such inquiries may be kept up for a few
moments or for several minutes. Indeed I have
been to "parties" where I was kept the entire time
answering questions about persons with whom the
other guests had associated me.*

The Ainu accompanies his inquiries with wishes
of good fortune to his interlocutor, to his wife and
family and relatives, to his native place. We also
wish well. "I hope you are in good health," we

---

* At one time in one resort inquiry always fell upon my saddle
horse. Any pronounced fad or pastime is a boon to your community, giving them something to talk to you about. My mare
is dead and the best substitute I can offer for her, I find, is a prospective "trip." "Where are you going now?" or "I hear you
are off again," is an easy conversational opening.

say, "I trust your mother has been better this winter."

Observations on personal comfort may be as effective in precluding intimacy as addressing a person as one of a family group. "Don't stand—"* —"Do rest yourself"—"Don't trouble"—"Don't rise"—"I hope you haven't taken cold"—"You aren't getting tired, are you?" or bored?—"*Za-gono?*" (Wagogo for "How have you slept?")[23]— all are formulas of barricade as well as expressions of solicitude. Perhaps in these cases humanity as a whole is the buffer group. Formulas about minding smoking or riding backwards or being in the way are similarly based on a sense of humanity and an obliviousness of the individual. *Petits soins*, little attentions, small courtesies, have something of the same character. To offer a woman a chair or a man a match or a cigar or, if you are a M'kikúyu[24] or lived a century ago, snuff, or, if a M'ganda, some of your coffee-berries to chew,[25] is a politeness that may help to make further personal attention unnecessary. Courtly manners are the readiest of guaranties against having to make unwonted social effort. "I am always polite

* "Don't sit," it may be in Samoa or in Zululand where sitting or squatting is the posture of respect. (Brown, p. 412; Leslie, David, *Among the Zulus* and *Amatongas*, p. 205. Glasgow, 1875.)

because it is so much trouble to be rude," writes a gentleman of the old school.[26]

Easy as "conversational openings," "small talk," and "good manners" may have rendered a meeting, freeing it of the dangers of personality, breaking it off is apt to be difficult. How many persons do not know when to say good-bye. Leave-taking seems to involve a sudden disquieting access of consciousness of the other personality. Hence leave-taking is very apt to be ceremonious. To say good-bye Papuans put on a mat or smear themselves with river mud and set to wailing.* Before leaving, a group of Abipones will say each in turn: "*Ma chik kla leyà?*" "Have we not talked enough?" "*Kla leyà,*" says the last one to speak and then they all rise up together.[27] "You stay and watch," says a Fijian on leaving. "Yes, and you voyage."[28] "So glad to have had this glimpse of you," we say, or we elaborate excuses for leaving or resort to various subterfuges about meeting again. "*Tamtâra,*"† "*roaroa,*"‡ "*au revoir,*" or "*auf*

---

* Wollaston tells how, on the departure of their party, a New Guinea native friend caught looking for tins in the vacated camp burst into tears and heartrending sobs "which changed in a moment, when he caught my eye, into a shout of laughter." (Wollaston, A. F. R., *Pygmies and Papuans*, p. 247. New York, 1912.)

† Abipone for "I shall see you again." (Dobrizhoffer, ii, 138.)

‡ Fijian for "the morning of to-morrow." (Williams, i, 152).

wiedersehen," are shorter formulas. To keep from asking, "When shall I see you again?" or from planning for a reunion betokens unusual intimacy.

In all the crises of life intimacy between acquaintances is peculiarly guarded against,—perhaps because under emotional stress personality tends to assert itself. Hence the critical event is either ceremonially ignored as in the case of divorce or death, sometimes of birth, or formal announcements of it are made or notices sent out, and set expressions of interest or sympathy or formulas of acknowledgment are considered appropriate. Births and deaths, betrothals and marriages are announced in the United States by card or newspaper, by toasts, by crêpe on the door-knob, or by flags at half-mast. In other places there are other methods of notification. In Switzerland a birth is announced by flowers worn by a girl of the family, a bouquet at her breast for a girl, another in her hand for a boy.[29] In the royal families of Europe cannon are fired as a birth notice or holidays or pardons proclaimed. To announce a death the Sinhalese send out a lock of hair cut from the head of the dead and twisted round a small stick, all wrapped in a leaf or a bit of cloth.[30] In Uganda both birth and death notices are given by drum-beats.[31] Ceremonial notices usually require an acknowledgment. To the friend who has become "engaged" or a "happy parent," a letter of congratulation has to be written*; to one "bereaved by death," a letter of condolence. We wish a bridal couple joy. We send to "inquire for" the sick. We pass resolutions in honour of the dead or pay them "tributes" at memorial meetings or in the newspapers.

During crises the usual impersonal devices of companionship are also resorted to—presents, calls, entertainments. There are wedding presents and birth and birthday presents, initiation or graduation or first communion presents, presents to mourners, presents to the dead. There are betrothal and wedding visits, visits to women after childbirth, to the dying, to the grave. There are betrothal and wedding festivities, pregnancy parties, naming or christening parties, death or memorial feasts. But present-giving, "calling," and "entertaining" are by no means limited to the crises of life. On endless occasions we are called upon to perform these "social duties." Whether or not they express, as this term implies, a sense of social obligation, they undoubtedly manifest our

* Writing is always to the fore in crises, for many barriers to intimacy have been formulated for writing, more even than for speech. Compare any "guide to correspondence" or "complete letter writer" with our published guides to conversation.

instinct of gregariousness. In varying measure
they betray apprehension too on the part of their
performers of personal relationships and they may
usually be suspected of being designed to preclude
intimacy or to substitute for it. From this point
of view it may be well to particularize a little
under separate headings in regard to these much
used parts of the social machinery, parts which in
all social codes from the Confucian classics to
contemporaneous books on etiquette receive considerable attention.

IX

PERHAPS the most iconoclastic organization formed in our day has been a New York society called the "Spugs," "The Society for the Prevention of Useless Giving." Its very organization indicates how grave the revolt against making presents is felt to be. Presents are so much a manifestation of sociability that the risk in not making them of being thought unsocial can only be lessened or offset by taking it with others. Unsociable together, declare the Spugs, we become sociable, as it were. It is plain enough that no Spug is willing to be considered unsocial. But to what extent is he or she consciously revolutionary? What presents do they really account useless? Birthday presents? Christmas presents? Engagement presents? Wedding presents? Presents made by guests, by the homing traveller, by seekers of political favour? Funeral presents? Votive offerings? Is it that the present has become to them an inadequate expression for the occasion or is it that the occasion itself has lost for them its significance? Or perhaps the Spugs are merely poor ethnologists, failing to realize the true usefulness of presents.

Whenever people think in terms of crises and act up to them presents have an important social function. For the chief participants they take the edge off the crisis and to outsiders they permit participation in the situation by enabling them to take part in the only way they care to—impersonally. They depersonalize what might otherwise be a trying moment. Like ceremonial of all kinds, ceremonial giving gratifies our instinct for gregariousness without the risk of intimacy. Presents may say even less than words. The chief who contributes a woman to the spirit harem of his deceased colleague is under no obligation to make any further expression of condolence. The kinsman who contributes to the raising of the bride-price or the friend of the family who sends the bride a wedding present is thereby relieved of even wishing the couple joy.

Grumbling over having to make such a present is, I surmise, merely a piece of modern discontent. In one of the Latin comedies there is, to be sure, a rather slurring reference to present-making. But it is not Geta who complains over having to make

a wedding present to the bride of his master's son,
not to speak of the prospect of being hit again for
other presents when she bears a child or when the
time comes for the child to be initiated. It is
Davus, the man from whom Geta is engaged in
collecting a bad debt,[1] and Davus may be suspected, like other malcontents, of taxing social conditions with his personal grievance.* In societies
that are neither Roman nor modern we really
never hear of such complaints. Take the Todas for
example. Who ever heard of a Toda complaining
over the buffaloes he must contribute to the funeral
services of certain relatives or over the *tinkanik
paum ûlpimi*, "we give a piece of money to the
purse," the rupee given by the family of a betrothed boy at the death of any member of the
family of his *fiancée?*[2] Take our colonial forebears.
The family of the deceased appears to have
lavished funeral gloves and scarfs and rings upon
attendant mourners and yet I find in the letters or
memoirs of the period no evidence of regret over
such displays of generosity.

Presents are useful not only in formal crises.

* Nevertheless there may have been some genuine Spug sentiment in Rome. Otherwise how are we to explain that provision
in the *XII Tables* against burying gold with the dead, quite as
remarkable a proscription as that of not sending flowers to
funerals.

They serve as buffers in emergencies. When a rupture of customary relations is imminent they may be depended upon to placate or appease—an irascible god, a jealous wife, an acquaintance quick to feel aggrieved. Peace offerings are a favourite way out too after the jar has occurred. They smooth past the jolt, they mend the break. Again and again the disturbance caused by social "breaks" is righted by a present. During his initiation a New Britain youth is expected to avoid most carefully his kinswomen; but if he have the bad luck to meet one of them in the bush he must hand over to her anything he happens to have with him. This forfeit his friends have subsequently to redeem for him, he being in disgrace until in this way they compensate the woman "for the shame of having met him."³ In the Islands of Torres Straits to call relatives by marriage by name is taboo. The man who inadvertently does so feels ashamed and his relative feels insulted; but the feelings of both may be relieved by a present of "some good thing."* If a Blackfoot

---

* *R. C. A. E. T. S.*, v, 143; vi, 99. The taboo is on women as well as men; but although the women break it frequently, the conciliatory present is not expected of them. It would mean utter impoverishment. As an illustration of the double standard the instance is not rare; but as an illustration of a greater lack of conventionality in women than in men it is rare indeed.

Indian appeared, however unintentionally, in the presence of his mother-in-law, it placed her in such an embarrassing position that he had to make amends by giving her a horse. [4]

When the jar in intercourse is due not to a social *faux pas*, but to absence, present-making is also of service. When Andamanese meet after prolonged absence they exchange whatever they happen to have in their hands*—bows, arrows, nautilus shells. [5] We recall how presents are made elsewhere by the homecoming traveller. Perhaps the present sent a host by his departed guest is also prompted in part by the desire to ease off the break in their relationship, ceremonial though it be. Analogously, in times of crisis, the present, I have no doubt, is a kind of shock absorber, diverting attention from the event itself, from death, let us say, or from growing up or from getting married.

That a present may be a bond as well as a buffer I am well aware. A present may establish a tie between giver and recipient, conveying in a kind of magical way something of the one to the other.†

* The rest of their behaviour is of interest. Without going through any other form of greeting, they gaze speechless at each other for some time, as much as half an hour; then the younger of the two, making some commonplace remark "to break the ice," says the ethnographer, they proceed to exchange the latest news.

† This may be the reason why present-making between the sexes is restricted. We read, for example, that "unmarried ladies

Betrothal or marriage presents exchanged between bride and groom may have this meaning and perhaps presents between host and guest and presents to the dead. But in all these instances the present is suggested by the feeling that there is a gap to be bridged over, the gap between the sexes, between members of different families or tribes or countries, between the living and the dead. What else is the present itself but an attempt to bridge the gap, a timid little approach to a personal relationship, pathetic enough at times, by those who know not the ways to intimacy?

---

ought not to accept presents from gentlemen who are neither related nor engaged to them." (Ward, p. 392.) Again, that "presents made by a married lady to a gentleman should be in the name of both herself and her husband." (Duffey, p. 150.) —To be sure the restriction appears at times to be economic. A lady is told, for example, that she "should not be under obligation to a man for presents that plainly represent a considerable money value" (Morton, p. 206), the idea being, I suppose, that her favours are purchasable. But this idea may be secondary, superimposed upon the original idea of sympathetic magic.

X

CALLING

PRESENTS are a natural appanage to another conspicuous expression of the gregarious instinct, the visit. Visits to the dwellings of the gods or of their human representatives, priests or chiefs, are almost always accompanied by presents. Among us, although turkeys are sent once a year to the White House and miscellaneous presents are received there from time to time, presents to statesmen are now as a rule discountenanced and sometimes even penalized as bribes. But in the churches votive offerings are still made or to the beggar at the portal alms are given, and even in Protestant churches the plate is passed.*

In less important or less conservative circles

---

* Why this difference between church and state? Perhaps it turns on the question of the return gift. A government official cannot make a return gift without injury to the commonwealth; but it seems to be held that the gods are not quite as restricted, although likely as not their favours to one may be at the cost of others. Then, too, unlike the gods, government officials are supposed to be on their job without the need of propitiation.

visits are independent of presents. They have, however, other ceremonial features. Describing them I shall have in mind merely the so-called "social call" in distinction to the wedding call, the call of inquiry, the call of condolence, etc., calls naturally partaking of the ceremonial of the occasion on which they are paid.—The "social call" has to be made during "calling hours," nowadays from half-past three to half-past six. A few years ago the hours were from two to four, as that interval interfered with "neither lunch nor the afternoon drive." In small towns, however, calling began as early as twelve o'clock.* In calling, the day of the week as well as the hour is of importance. A call should be paid on "the day at home" of the hostess,† or if a man is calling on a woman, on Sunday, after church or in the afternoon.¹ Exceptions to these rules I shall refer to later. A call must not last less than five or more than fifteen minutes. For paying it one's "best" or at least "second best" clothes must be worn, "a calling dress or costume more elegant than that worn for walking or for shopping." Gentlemen wear "a black cut-away, or a frock-coat, dark trousers,

* Ward, p. 67.   The "social call" was once called the "morning call."

† A call upon any other day "seems to denote no wish to see her." (*Ib.*, p. 62.)   But cp. *Manners and Social Usage*, p. 7.

silk necktie (black is in the best taste), and a medium or neutral shade of gloves."[2] A man calling in his "business suit" at least apologizes for it. However they are dressed, "gentlemen leave their umbrellas, overcoats, and overshoes in the hall; but take their hats and sticks with them into the drawing-room, unless they are calling on old friends."[3] Except possibly with old friends too, the call is characterized by certain formulas of speech as well as by certain clothes, and a more or less restricted set of topics of conversation is employed. Conversational openings and polite inquiries appear to special advantage in calling. A call has to be "returned" and returned within a given period. In returning it "the exact etiquette of the person who has left the first card" should be observed.[4] Calling is held to be a preliminary, and in this we see its most marked ceremonial aspect, indispensable to further social intercourse. "You can hardly invite people to your house until you have called and have left a card. To stop an acquaintance, one has but to stop leaving cards. It is thus done quietly but securely."[5]

Calling, like present-making, is subject to careful regulation between the sexes, and between those of different ages or of different castes. Women do not pay calls on men, "no lady leaves

her own card upon a gentleman."[6]   And yet
calling appears to be more obligatory for women
than for men.   "In case a man is legitimately
prevented, by business cares, from paying calls
or leaving his cards in person, it is proper for his
wife or mother or sister, or other near relative,* to
leave or send his card with her own."[7] Sometimes
a man wishes to call in person. He may not "call
upon a lady," however, "unless he has first received
permission to do so."[8] Nor does he ask in calling
for the young ladies only. It is indeed incorrect
for a very young lady to invite a gentleman to
call.[9]

Younger women are not only restricted in the
matter of calls by men, but also in connection with
calls by elder women. In that annual exchange of
calls certain authorities consider necessary to the
continuance of an acquaintance, it is the junior
who has to pay the first call. Under other circumstances any doubt arising as to who should call
first is determined by seniority. It is always the

* "Only the women of his own household, or a relative with
whom he habitually pays visits, can thus represent a man by
proxy." (Morton, p. 32.) His proxies are sometimes neglectful
according to this authority. "'Solid men' would go 'into society'
far more frequently and with greater alacrity if they felt assured
that the way had been paved with their own visiting cards, well
laid in place by the deft fingers of their skilful women folk, who
have left no flaw in the mosaic of social proprieties." (*Ib.*, p. 35.)

privilege of the senior to wait to be called upon. She has the privilege too under certain circumstances of leaving cards upon her junior without asking to see her, a performance in the younger woman nothing less than a gross affront. Then the truly aged may cease from calling altogether.[10]

Caste affects calling. An "inferior" does not call upon his or her "superior," at least without a special invitation.* "It is not the correct thing to call first upon people in a higher social position than one's own."[11] Even where the difference in position is slight, it is the lady higher in rank or more "prominent in fashion" who pays the first call.[12]

Into the ceremonial of the "first call" enter many nice distinctions besides those of rank or age. "At places of summer resort, those who own their cottages call first upon friends who rent them; and those who rent, in turn, call upon each other according to the priority of arrival; while both those who own and those who rent call first upon friends arriving at the hotels."[13] But supposing

* Unless we consider, as perhaps we should, ecclesiastical or political "audiences," church hours, or public receptions in the light of calls.

Herbert Spencer considers that calling originated as an act of homage. It was a form of propitiation by the "inferior" of the "superior."

both ladies arrived at the same time to occupy both of them rented villas? Then "the lady whose house is in the city nearest to the watering place would assuredly feel herself at liberty to make the first call if she desired to make the acquaintance of her neighbour, provided they had both rented the villas for the first time that season. If not, the one who has been the longest occupant calls first, without reference to the distance of their respective cities."[14]   In the autumn, home from the summer resort, those who return first call first.[15]

Calling plays an important part in the practice of hospitality. It may be that the stranger is not invited to an "entertainment" until he has called "to pay his respects." (I know one woman who says she never asks a man to dinner unless he has first called, and I have read of hostesses who make in this connection a seasonal demand.*) Then unless the guest calls† after the entertainment, he may not be invited to another. He must call promptly, too, certainly within three days. To this dinner call, as it is known among us, a very special

---

* "Gentlemen should not expect to receive invitations from ladies with whom they are only on terms of formal visiting, until the yearly or autumnal call has been made, or until their cards have been made to represent themselves." (Ward, p. 79.)

† In China and in some places in the United States he may send or leave cards.

value appears to attach. It continues to be paid by persons who pay calls of no other kind. Important, however, as it is, the late hostess is expected not to be "at home" when it is paid. "For this reason persons who wish to leave cards only, call within the prescribed three days, as they are then sure of not being admitted where the customs of society are understood."[16]

With us "tea" is the only "refreshment" offered to a caller; elsewhere the refection or, as in Japan, the manner of serving it, is more elaborate. In Hayti I once had to drink champagne during an early morning call and once in Sicily an after-dinner *liqueur* on an empty stomach. In Manila certain native fruits were always offered to me when I called. During the piñon nut season in New Mexico I have noticed that both Indians and Mexicans take for granted in their callers an exhaustless capacity for piñon nuts, frequently a not unpleasant assumption. And just so any traveller, I suspect, is sure to have stories of what he has had set before him during his calls upon the natives. Even among us a sojourner would find that when the day at home had been magnified into an afternoon reception it was the correct thing "to have several varieties of delicate and pretty cakes, and several kinds of sandwiches and bread and butter, also salted almonds, candies, litchi nuts, or other dainty trifles on the afternoon tea-table."[17]

Entertainment other than food or drink may also be offered to callers. "It is the correct thing: To darken the windows and light the rooms by artificial light at a large and handsome reception, also to decorate the house with flowers and to hire a band of musicians, if the hostess wish to do so." Also: "To have a small informal dance succeed an afternoon tea or reception, notifying beforehand the guests who are to remain and take part in it and perhaps asking others to remain, on the spur of the moment."[18] In India too dancing is a feature in calling. A distinguished man about to call upon another engages to accompany him a troupe of *quasi* temple dancers.

Calling, like so many of the customs we have been noting, is becoming obsolete; but I have had the good fortune to observe it in one of the few places where its practice is still vigorous, in Washington. Washington has not yet entered upon the decadent stage of calling, the stage of leaving cards or even mailing them. The Washington call must be made in person. Cards must be left, however, whether the hostess is seen or not. They are deposited on the hall table or, in hotels or

apartment houses, in the letter box in the office.*
A row of baskets is sometimes provided for these
cards outside the door of the hotel parlour within
which a row of ladies stand to "receive." Ladies
who receive together in this way may be covered
rapidly, but even calls in private houses may be
"done" without much loss of time. From thirty
to fifty calls may be made of an afternoon by the
expert providing, as she puts it, she has luck, *i. e.*
she does not find everyone in. She has of course
drawn up her list with forethought and she is
punctilious in timing each call. She keeps within
a safe range of conversation in order not to be
beguiled into exceeding her allotted time or into
overdrawing upon the energy she needs for accom-
plishing her round. The fund of energy she starts
with seems, however, at times to increase rather
than lessen; each call done gives her, I take it, a
stimulating sense of having acquired merit. At
any rate at the end of the three hours, however
tired she may be, her sense of accomplishment is
vastly satisfying. And so for several months
during the year the Washington resident pays her
daily round of calls, returning to the top of her

* "Should the lady of the house open the door herself, the card
must by no means be handed to her; it should be left as unob-
trusively as possible on the hall table or elsewhere." (*Manners
and Social Usages*, p. 13.)

list when she reaches the bottom of it,* a being more gregarious or more impersonal it were hard to find.

In Washington those who called most, I noticed, went "out" least, and there seemed to be little or no relation at any rate between calling and "going out"; but according to those books on American etiquette I have had to cite, my opportunities for observation at first hand having been locally limited, the relations between calls and entertainments in the country at large are close. Not only does the call and the call alone qualify you to be invited to entertainments, but "after an interchange of cards, the acquaintance drops, unless followed by an invitation upon one side or the other."[19]   In other words calling without the adjunct of entertaining does not firmly establish an acquaintance, calls being only "in part the bases upon which that great structure, society, mainly rests."[20]

---

* For in Washington the rule does not hold that "once an acquaintance is established, it is kept up by calling once a year." (*The Complete Hostess,* p. 311.)   In Washington "one's card left on the hall table at a reception or tea establishes the acquaintance for a year" only if the call is not meanwhile returned.   Returned, it must be in turn returned.   Also it is a question in Washington whether attending a tea counts as a call.   Among the most scrupulous, *i.e.* in Congressional circles, it does not count.

XI

ENTERTAINING

"THERE'S no use in coming to your party," one sometimes hears from the social rebel, "I shan't see anything of you. One never does of one's hostess, or of anyone else, that's the worst of parties." True, but why make any point of it? Why suggest that entertainments should be for the sake of personal relationships? They bring people together, but it is their very nature to keep personalities apart. They are essentially devices for gregariousness and for gregariousness only, for gregariousness safeguarded against personal relationship. To expect them to yield opportunities for intimacy is peculiarly modern and, if I may say so, ignorant and rather silly. A brief survey of the leading forms of entertaining may show how irrational is the grievance of those who, disappointed on this score, "don't like society."

Perhaps the simplest form of "society" is the procession or the review. It prevails in royal and in ecclesiastical circles. Sir Richard Burton, that inimitable traveller, gives a graphic account of a procession he witnessed at the court of Dahomi. "The Caboceers [head men] were followed by the companies, of which the first was that of the Ahaujito or singers and of the Hunto or drummers. · . . The distinguishing mark was the large-tail 'chauri,' with a man's jawbone above the handle. They were preceded by nine 'fancy flags,' adorned with all manner of figures, animate and inanimate, cut out of coloured cloth and sewn upon the plain ground. These were followed by . . . eight human crania dished up on small wooden bowls like bread-plates, at the top of very tall poles. . . . The Achi, or bayoneteers, were headed by their commander in a man-o'-war's cap, about twenty in number. . . . Followed a few carbineers, whose half-shaven heads showed them to be slaves of the palace: they are known as Zo-hu-nun—'Fire at the foe's front.' A white flag with a blue anchor at the end of a waving red stripe denoted the Gan'u'nlan Company, the 'Conquerors of all animals,' so called from the size of their guns, which are expected to kill, not to wound: forming part of the artillery with the Agbáryá, or blunderbuss men, they are chosen for size and strength, and much prefer themselves to the commonalty of the army. They followed a tattered Jack and a fancy flag, and their chiefs bowed to us, whilst the men, resting the butt upon the ground, fired resonant charges."[1]

A review is a favourite way not only with African monarchy but with government everywhere of entertaining distinguished guests. A religious procession on a Saint's day may be accounted an analogous form of hospitality, a form that Church and State, even if at other times they go separate ways, usually unite in celebrating.* But political or ecclesiastical parades are not limited to entertaining distinguished travellers or saints; they occur on a great variety of occasions. Nor is the parade or procession itself as a form of sociability confined to State or Church. There are university or school processions, guild or labour processions, funeral and wedding and "coming out" marches, the walk in to dinner, woman suffrage processions, and, most recent of all, peace parades.—Parade ceremonial consists of marching together, usually with music to facilitate keeping step or to inspire in the marchers the same emotion at the same moment, and the carrying of banners, standards, or insignia, and of the elimination, more or less compulsory, of verbal communication.

---

* Mgr. Lavelle and Mayor Mitchell, for example, head together the St. Patrick's Day parade in New York City.

Almost as perfect an expression of gregariousness as marching is dancing, or at least certain
forms of dancing. Dancing figures in fact in processions. In the parade during the So-sin Custom
held in honor of deceased Dahoman royalty,
"seven troubadour women, holding horse-tails and
twirling flags in their left hands," assisted by
another band of fifty women, "danced long and
violently before the King."[2] In the Abipone
funeral parade, the women were said to "go leap-
ing like frogs."[3] After the engulfing of the
Egyptians, when Miriam led forth the Jewish
women, she danced before them. The military
"goose step" may be called, I suppose, a dance
step. Even detached from the parade, dancing
has traits in common with it—movement to
rhythm and more or less of a taboo on speech,
particularly in primitive dancing. Dances are
even more widespread than parades, occurring on
an even greater variety of occasions and at
assemblies of all kinds.* When their husbands
were campaigning it was incumbent upon the Tshi
tribeswomen to dance.[4] *Débutante* dances[5] and
dances at tribal initiations and at weddings are
very common. The modern ballet was given its

---

* In rare instances dancing seems to be spontaneous. The
Veddas are said to dance for pleasure like a child.

impulse, it is said, in Italy at an entertainment
to celebrate the marriage of Isabella of Aragon
and Galeazzo, Duke of Milan.[6]   Many peoples
besides the Abipones dance at funerals.   Burton
saw fifty of the queens of Dahomi dancing before
the shrine of their royal father-in-law during the
memorial services in his honour.[7] Outside of Italy
and Dahomi dancing has ever been a popular
court entertainment.   At religious gatherings too
dancing is apt to be a feature.   Among some of the
Moslem sects and some of the early Christian,
in Shinto, in the cults of the Hindu gods, among
the Shakers, with the priesthoods of the Ewes
and Tshis, of the Awemba, and in fact of in-
numerable tribes, dancing is a condition of
"possession."*

Chanting or singing often accompanies dancing;
but it is often too a separate form of entertainment.
The funeral dirge is universal.   The serenade of
courtship and the wedding song are common.
The gods have their holy singers and in almost all
churches ritual is intoned or sung.   There are also
court singers.   The *conteur* once kept by every
Turkish Pasha told his story in rhythm.[8]   At
Benin it was a chief's wives who sang in his

---

* May we not consider possession gregariousness at its
intensest?

honour, each lady being famous for some particular song.[9] I have often heard of an American singer asking permission to sing at the musicales given periodically at the White House.

Singing has ever been considered a social accomplishment. The Ainu returned from abroad chants the account he gives his friends of his travels.[10] The Akikúyu welcome strangers with a song.[11] Every evening the Bororo chief *sings* his orders for the following day.[12] The Euahlayi of New South Wales[13] *sings* his riddles.* To be socially qualified the early Victorian damsel was taught to sing, and in many an old-time novel her friends are assumed to be pleased to listen to her. She was a successor, so to speak, of the mediæval minstrel, singing after instead of during dinner. Minstrelsy at feasts is very common. At a party given to the Routledges by the chief of the Akikúyu, two young warriors each sang a solo, all joining in the chorus and the ladies at the close applauding.[14] There was singing at Chinese "drinking entertainments"—commonly a few lines from one of the pieces of the *Shih King* expressing a sentiment appropriate to the occasion.[15] A few

---

* Telling riddles is in itself a form of entertainment. No longer very popular among us except in childhood, it is a favourite pastime of savages and of peasants. Like proverbs or aphorisms or quotations, riddles enable a conversation to be quite impersonal.

years ago at a luncheon given to us, a party of
visiting American politicians, by the Japanese
Minister of War, the Marquis Ito, famous among
statesmen, sang to us verses of his own written in
our honour.* On another occasion, after dinner
in Japanese style,† our hosts entertained us with a
Japanese play acted by the leading geisha company
of Tokio. We too take our dinner guests to play
or opera. Elsewhere the feast itself has been
enlivened by the drama.

Into the religious origins of the drama we need
not go. The last trace of its ecclesiastical character disappeared when women and children were no
longer excluded from it. But it persists without

* The charm of this naïve performance was all the greater
because other native ways had been so carefully hidden from us
by our hosts; but on some of us the charm, I fear, was lost, on
those of us not familiar, even ethnographically, with minstrelsy at
meals.

† We sat on cushions on the floor, women and men in different
rooms. The elderly Kentuckian next to me had rheumatism and
suffered considerably from her bent knees. There were other
incongruities about the dinner. A Virginian put her chop-sticks
in her hair. On the other side of me sat a charming Japanese *girl*.
Japanese girls do not dine out and she was the only one we had
met. Her mother was a lady of high position and with very advanced ideas. Because of them she had been subject to much
criticism by her countrymen. When her critics heard of the
unwonted presence of her daughter at our dinner party together
with the indecent feat of one of the guests, did they not exclaim,
I wonder, "This shows what will happen if we let girls go out in
the American fashion; they will begin to put their *hashi* in their
hair!"

8

the backing of the Church or even at times in the face of the Church because it is such an adequate satisfaction of the gregarious instinct, a satisfaction both ample and safe. Without any personal communication the audience has endless opportunities to feel the same emotion and in its laughter or applause, in its hissing or cat-calling, to express it unanimously.

In games we find the gregarious instinct again expressing itself, notably and directly in games based on co-operation, but also in games of competition. In both its types the game encourages association and diverts attention away from the personalities engaged in it to itself.

But of all forms of gregariousness, eating or drinking together is by far the commonest and most ubiquitous. Few entertainments are complete without "refreshments," and very often the refection constitutes the whole entertainment. During the feast or drinking bout no distractions are provided; even conversation may be bad form. The Japanese and other Orientals eat in silence. When silence is not expected of diners-out, the talk itself may be subject to restrictions. "Nothing should be said which can hurt any one's feelings," states the writer of *Manners and Social Usages*, adding that "politics, religion, and the

stock market" are generally ruled out.[16]   The
proscription of these particular topics of conversation is not common enough, perhaps, for reasons
already noted, to warrant this observation; but it is
quite true that the range of conversation is narrower at the dinner table than elsewhere. On the
other hand conversation of some kind there must
be. A silence is felt to be very embarrassing, and
the success of a dinner is judged of "by the manner
in which conversation has been sustained. If it
has flagged often, it is considered a proof that the
guests have not been congenial; but if a steady
stream of talk has been kept up, it shows that
they have smoothly amalgamated as a whole."[17]

Many details of conduct besides sustaining
conversation or conversing on appropriate topics
go to make up table manners. Given the close
contacts a common meal involves, an elaborate
ceremonial is to be expected. For much of its
detail as well as for the great stress laid upon its
observance I must refer the reader to more systematic books on etiquette—unless he is enterpris-
ing enough to analyse his own experiences. As to
the ceremonial of feasting in general we may
observe that as in other forms of gregariousness
caste, age, and sex receive much consideration.
Kings, we have noted, do not eat with commoners,

nor servants with their masters. But even slighter distinctions in social position are recognized at dinners. In this country they are recognized most obviously, perhaps, in Washington. Here a Cabinet Minister walks out to dinner before a Senator; a Justice of the Supreme Court sits on the right of the hostess unless the presence of an Ambassador has compelled a move to the left; it is the wife of the Representative who has served longest who has to make the "first move to go" after dinner. Outside of the Capital these particular distinctions are comparatively ignored and plutocratic distinctions are more to the fore, not conspicuously, however, for the simple reason that in many circles hostesses are inclined not to "mix" people at dinner. Dinner guests, they hold, "should be of the same standing."[18] "They need not necessarily be friends, or even acquaintances; but, as at a dinner people come into closer contact than at any other kind of a party, those only should be invited to meet one another who move in the same class or circles."[19] Within my memory in New York City the fashionable and unfashionable were rarely if ever invited to dine together.

Nor at one time were the young and the old.* When *débutantes* and "married people" did begin

* See Chapter XV. for the grouping at table by age-class.

to dine together, age took precedence. "In proceeding from the drawing-room to the dining-room, the younger fall back until the older have advanced."[20] Dinner announced, "stand back for all the married dames to pass out before you," writes the Young Lady's Friend, "and if a gentleman, wishing to escort you, attempt to lead you out before them, draw back, and do not let him."[21] At table, the Friend continues, "try to seat yourself among the least important portion of the company."[22] As for the seating of seniors at table, "a host waits upon the oldest lady,"* and the hostess is escorted by the eldest gentleman.[23]

The relations between the sexes are carefully regulated at dinners, when they dine together at all. In many communities the principle underlying "stag" dinners and ladies' luncheons is unbroken, men and women either eating in different places or the women eating after the men. A Uripiv† Islander who eats with a woman runs the risk of a mysterious death.[24] A New York man I know tells me that in a "business men's restaurant" he always avoids a table where women are sitting, and yet this same man is not at all

* Or, let us note, upon "the greatest stranger."
† New Hebrides.

averse, in the evening, to commensality. Is it because at mixed dinners he has little or no option about his relations to the sex? At mixed dinners men have to take the women out and the sexes alternate at the table,* unless a hostess wishes to display the fact that she has at command more than enough men to go round. But men do not like to sit next to men at dinner, even to gratify the vanity of their hostess. Women are even more averse to sitting next to women. It is only after dinner that such an alignment of the sexes is acceptable, and then only for a short period. Not to have a man come up to talk to her after the men have come in from the smoking-room is embarrassing to a lady.

*That they are expected to talk first on one side and then the other, as the table "turns," we may note as another provision of the ceremonial conversation of the feast.

XII

BETWEEN THE SEXES

S EX is one of the two* greatest sources of difference between its members society has to
apprehend.   It deals with the disturbing factor in
its characteristically simple, unconscious way.   It
separates men and women as much as possible, or
when because of passion or of economic necessity
or convenience actual separation is impossible or
difficult, it raises barriers between them.

In every society the separation of the sexes is
more or less thoroughly marked.   No Vedda may
come in contact with any women of his own age except his wife, ¹ a restriction observed in many savage
tribes.†   " Male and female should not sit together

---

* Age, of course, is the other.   See pp. 176 ff.
† The proprieties of the haremlik may be observed even in a
communal cave.   In a Vedda cave dwelling "the woman may
always be seen at exactly the same spot, and when the men come
in they sit or lie beside their wives, keeping to that part of the
cave floor that belongs to them as carefully as though there
was a partition dividing it from that of their neighbours."
(Seligmann, *The Veddas*, p. 86.)

in the same apartment, nor have the same stand
or rack for their clothes, nor use the same towel or
comb, nor let their hands touch in giving and receiving," prescribes the *Lî Kî*.[2] In Corea the mere
touch of a strange man has caused a father, it is
said, to kill his daughter, or a wife to kill herself.[3]
Out-of-doors a Miridite girl of Albania speaks to a
man unrelated to her at the risk of losing her
reputation,[4] a calamity few girls care to survive.
Dobrizhoffer relates that one day after his arrival
in Paraguay he played in the road on the flute.
The girls gathered to listen; but as soon as the
youths came up the girls, every one, disappeared.[5]
The English girl of the fifteenth century was put
on her guard in rhyme:

"Aqweynte thee not with eche man that gooth bi the
    strete;
Though ony man speke to thee, Swiftli thou him
    grete
Lete him go bi the way: bi him that thou ne stonde."[6]

In the United States to-day a mother sometimes
tells her daughter not to speak to any strange man
in the street—except a policeman; and it was once
thought bad form for a girl to go "buggy-riding"
with a man or in town to be seen with one in a cab.
Only a few years ago a New York girl told me that
having to drive home late in the evening in a

"strange" cab and without a chaperone, she required her escort to sit on the box with the driver.

There are in most communities certain places assigned to one sex into which the other may not venture, or venture only at their peril. No Aeneze of good reputation would sit down in that corner of the women's part of the tent called the *roffe*. "Your sitting place is the *roffe*," is said to a man you despise.[7] Corean boys were taught that it was shameful to set foot at all in the women's part of the house, and in Seoul men breaking the law requiring them to leave the streets to the women from eight P.M. to one A.M. were severely punished.[8] A New Guinea woman found anywhere near the place where the feast of the sacred bullroarer is being celebrated is taken and put at the disposition of the assembled men.[9] New Hebrides men also violate women who eavesdrop around the club house of their secret society.[10] London or New York clubmen are likely to make "insulting remarks," I am told, about women who even look into their club windows. A man who addresses a girls' school or joins a ladies' sewing circle is expected to feel discomposed. "How do you like being the only man?" he is asked.

The sexes are apt to be separated in their economic pursuits, in their pastimes, and in their

social interests and activities in general. In
North-western Siam iron is worked only by the
women and they only pole the boats.[11] Nāgas
who touch women's weaving or pottery tools are
punished.[12] Among the Akikúyu only the men
herd the goats. The long distance carries of fire-
wood are made only by the women and of a big
load men say, "This is a very heavy load, it is fit
to be carried by a woman, not by a man."[13] In
Uganda hunting is an activity improper for a
woman, more improper here even than in other
countries. A woman who kills any animal or
catches them for others to kill is considered unfit
for society.[14] Reading as well as hunting has been
taboo to women. "Some Stoicks indeed there are
who will not allow any Books to Womankind,"
writes a sixteenth-century Englishman.[15] Coryat,
the seventeenth-century English traveller, records
that until he went to Venice he had never seen
women on the stage, and even in Venice there were
no women in the audience except courtesans, and
they sat apart and wore masks.[16] "It is not
comlye for a woman to practise feates of armes,
ridinge, playing at tenise,* wrastling, and manye

---

* Fashions at least change. Not long ago I heard that great
evangelist of our day, Billy Sunday, declare that tennis was not
to his liking, it was "too girlified." To that description one of

other thynges that beelonge to men," asserted one
of the sixteenth-century courtiers of Urbino.[17]
"I beleve musicke," he also says, "together with
many other Vanities is mete for women, . . . but
not for men that be men in dede."[18] In Central
Australia a man is not allowed to attend the
memorial death service of a woman.[19] A Massim
woman may not enter or even approach the
bolabola or circle of stones where the men sit to
talk.[20] In the fifteenth century the English youth
was cautioned to be reticent in the presence of
ladies.

> "In chambur among ladyes bryghth
> Kepe thy tonge and spende thy syghth."[21]

"Outside affairs should not be talked of inside the
threshold of the women's apartments, nor inside or
women's affairs outside it,"[22] prescribes the *Lî Kî*.
Furthermore, "Male and female, without the in-
tervention of the matchmaker, do not know each
other's name."[23]

Separation of the sexes is also assured through
other forms of social separation. Social barriers
based on differences in age, in culture and religion,
in economic or political class, in kinship and race,

---

his followers, a tennis devotee, audibly demurred. "I know,"
said the preacher, "Rody plays tennis and he's no sissie."

all figure in exaggerated form the moment sex itself figures. The merest glance at marriage restrictions shows this condition. Even when marriage within one's own age-class is not required by law or custom, how misled is the girl who marries an old man,* how ludicrous the young man who falls in love with an old woman. With any married woman who is his junior, an Andamanese is forbidden direct communication.[24] Unless a woman unrelated to him is "very much his senior," an American is advised by at least one writer on etiquette not to offer her valuable presents.[25] In fact so efficient a barrier between the sexes does a difference in age appear that among simple people it is sometimes simulated as a device for separation. Masai warriors have to salute married women with "*Endakwenya,*" "O old ladies!"[26] As soon as one of our girls marries, do not her male contemporaries think of her as much "older" and has one not heard persons describe themselves as "an *old* married man," or "an *old* married woman"?

In parts of Europe in the Middle Ages marriage

---

* Gerontocracy and marriage by purchase (whether the bride is bought or whether she marries for money) are factors tending to legitimatize or conventionalize this type of misalliance. The monopoly of girls by the Elders may also force juniors into marriage with older women, aging widows.

with a Jew was punishable by death, nor did Jewish law recognize marriage with an unbeliever.
The Moslem has been forbidden to marry the
Christian; the Catholic, the Protestant; the Angli-
can, the Dissenter. Caste may be as set against
mixed marriages as religion. In China actors,
policemen, and boatmen must marry within their
class.[27] An Aeneze never marries his daughter to
a *szona*, *i. e.*, a blacksmith or a saddler,* or to a
descendant of a *szona* family.[28] Everywhere a
non-celibate priesthood tends to be endogamous.
Marriage between slaves and free women is always forbidden and other sex relations between
them are apt to be more severely penalized than
illegitimate relations between others. A Teutonic
woman who had intercourse with a slave was likely
to be killed. A Guatemalan who married a slave
became one. Among the Hovas of Madagascar
even the three classes of slaves do not intermarry.
Roman plebeians and patricians could not intermarry until 455 B.C. Such misalliances were punished in Sweden until the seventeenth century.[29]
Again and again European royalties have had to
forgo rank or position through marrying out of
their class, and in every civilized country marrying

---

* These workmen are always of another tribe, their occupation
being accounted degrading to an Aeneze.

beneath you involves in varying degree social disapproval or ostracism. There are few American girls, I surmise, who would at no time feel ashamed of having a man of an inferior social position make love to them.

Shame, a sense of disgrace, of blight, is also felt over the violation of endogamous rules of kinship or of race. Were a Pádam girl to demean herself by marrying out of her clan, sun and moon would refuse to shine, Dalton was once assured, and all labour would have to cease until by sacrifice and oblation the stain was washed away. A Bushman woman considers intercourse with any man not of her tribe degrading. The Baralongs, a Bechuana tribe, killed any of their women intimate with a European.[30] In sections of the United States marriage between whites and blacks has been prohibited. On the steamer on which I once travelled with a Congressional party to the Philippines were a bride and groom, she a New Englander and he a Filipino, a graduate of Harvard University and the son of a prominent Mestizo Judge in Manila. This bridal pair the members of our party, with but few exceptions, were not willing to meet, and later in Manila I learned that the members of the American Army and Navy Club were resolved to ostracize the young woman.

"We'll teach her," they said, "an American girl can't marry a Filipino."

Marriage aside, racial shyness or distrust is notably exaggerated by a difference of sex. In those parts of Borneo where it was believed that the sight of a white man caused illness, the men warned their wives not to approach the European traveller.[31] The headman of a New Guinea pygmy village resisted a bribe of three shining axes, writes Wollaston, to let his English visitors have merely a sight of the village women, hidden away in the jungle.[32] The Veddas do not allow visitors of any race to see their women. Even pedlars may not approach nearer than a quarter of a mile of their caves.[33] During a British inspection trip on the Burmese Chinese boundary, a Kakhyen chief was told that the officials were going to sleep in his house. Although resentful of the intrusion, all the chief asked for was time to get the women out of the way.[34] Burckhardt relates that the Bedouin women he met on the road would often ask him for flour or biscuit, but that they would never take it out of his hands. He had to set it down on the ground, behind their backs, and then withdraw from them a few paces.[35] In the South and South-West I have found American women afraid to

go walking alone on the chance of meeting a negro
or a Mexican.

But in addition to taboos of physical separation
or of exclusiveness, taboos of the imagination are
relied upon in separating the sexes,—conceptions
of the psychic or magical dangers of infidelity,
of the magical nature of chastity and its irre-
trievability, of the impurity of sexual intimacy,
and of the evil intrinsic in passion. An Aleut
woman believes that were she unfaithful to her
husband when he went hunting he would get no
game.[36] The wife of the Kayan camphor collector
believes that her infidelity would cause the trees
to be empty of camphor.[37] Elsewhere wives believe too that infidelity brings a husband disaster
of a magical kind called dishonour. An unchaste
sister as well as a faithless wife can spoil an Aleut's
hunt. Chastity in many another tribe has magical
potentialities. In the historical religions it is a
factor in the working of miracles.[38] Complementary to this view of chastity as an instrument for
magic is the notion that like any other instrument
it can be lost and lost once and for all, particularly
in the case of women. "In women honestye once
stained dothe never retourne again to the former
estate"[39]—not even through marriage. To Paul,
to Buddha, and to many another religious devotee

passion even in marriage is more than question-
able. "Let none imagine that we approve of sexual intercourse except for procreation!" exclaims
Father Jerome.[40] After conception, give to marriage "the sanctity of virginity," exhorts Mother
Eddy.[41]

The belief that feminine weakness or inferiority
is infectious* seems to be back of some of these
conceptions. This belief also accounts for the very
widespread taboos against women imposed upon
huntsmen and fishermen, upon magicians and
priests, upon warriors on the eve of professional
expeditions or enterprises. From time to time one
finds too that special precautions are taken against
catching femininity. Were a youth of Fraser's
Island to sit down on the stool a girl was sitting on
or had sat on, he believes he would sicken and die.[42]
Were a Maryborough Blackfellow woman to step
over anything belonging to a man, he would throw
it away.[43] In South Africa a man sleeping with
his wife must be careful not to touch her with
his right hand. Otherwise his strength as a warrior goes from him, he believes, and he will surely
be killed.[44] Among its editorial New Year wishes

---

* Male traits may be catching too. If an Australian girl ties
on a man's waist band, she becomes sterile. (Spencer & Gillen,
Native Tribes, p. 52, n. 1.)

this year one of the New York daily papers wished for manhood for an editor of a review of feminist bias. This editorial was shown to me by a man who frankly and solemnly said he felt his own manhood would be imperilled by any considerable interest in the affairs of women.

The conception of feminine weakness is but one of the many generalizations about women every society makes. "The tongues of women cannot be governed,"[45] say the Makololo. "The love of possessions is a woman's trait and not a brave's," said his grandmother to the Sioux boy, Hakadah, when she called upon him to offer up his pet dog in sacrifice.[46] Deprecating to her husband her failure to obey him and expose their infant daughter, a wife in one of the plays of Terence refers to her waywardness as characterized by "a woman's usual folly and miserable superstition."[47] In another play a testy husband exclaims: "What a thing it is that all women are set on the same thing and set against the same thing, and not one of them can you find an inch different from the bent of the rest."[48]

As barriers to personal relations these sex generalities are most efficient. Hence they are apt to be to the fore in the beginning of an acquaintanceship,* always a more or less formidable time, or whenever a personal relation becomes displeasing. "Just like a woman!" "How like a man!" exclaims the irritated man or woman. And the interpretation of motive or conduct in terms of sex is often a justification for slackness, an excuse for carelessness. Because women are all the same, it is not worth while to pay close attention to a given woman. Because a given man is like other men, much is not to be expected of him,—unless one is speaking in terms of chivalry, when too much cannot be expected of him.

Chivalry, based, as we have noted, on a generalization, that of inborn and ineradicable superiority, serves like other generalizations as a barrier between the sexes, a particularly strong barrier too. Good manners between the sexes are analogous barriers. They too are efficient, almost as efficient as avoidance practices. But often too they require avoidance. Ainu women are always taught to get out of the way of men on a path. If Tasmanians met a party of women on the trail, it was only polite of them to turn and go another way.⁴⁹ With us a man merely turns out for a woman. In

---

* And is not the beginning of intimacy between a man and a woman apt to be characterized by each conceiving that the other is an exception to his or her sex?

Uganda a woman may not hand a man anything
without first wrapping it in a bit of plantain leaf. [50]
It is good Ainu manners for women to wait to be
spoken to by men, [51] just as under certain circumstances it is polite among us for a man not to speak
first to a woman.

Individuals upon whom these taboos lie heavy,
the womanly woman, the man's man, are attrac-
tive to the opposite sex, not only for elemental
reasons, but because they are felt to be safe. Obviously they have no wish for assimilation, no
tendency to cross the self-protecting barriers of sex.
They will let the habits of the other sex alone.*

Fear of not being let alone accounts for the
otherwise strange brutality shown from time to
time by men towards intrusive women. We have
already noted how women trespassers may be
treated. Women pioneers in law or medicine or
politics† have also in case after case been subject
to injury or "insults." These "insults" ‡ have

* To be let alone is, I suggest, more desirable to simple people
than any "complementary difference of character," the effect
no doubt of sex taboos but, Crawley notwithstanding, never their
motive.

† Is it not therefore a prime tactical error for suffragists to
suggest in any way that woman suffrage will compel any change
in masculine habits or, for that matter, in feminine?

‡ Women, more conservative than men, are more open to
"insult." An insult is an outrage against one's habits and is not

been for the most part of an obscene nature, for men feel, more or less unconsciously, that women are vulnerable in questions of sex, because in their habits of chastity they in their turn are most loath to be disturbed. But in their other habits, too, women, like men, wish to be protected, and so they have been ever ready to be cut off from experiences unsettling to habits—from intercourse with the stranger or with the gods, from learning, from travel, from nature. To almost any demand that they live at second hand they have been compliant.*

Is not this desire to be unaffected by the opposite sex back of the insistent demand to safeguard the mystery of sex? You will destroy the mystery and so the charm of sex, it is urged, if you let women do *all* the things men do. Men will treat women like men; they will forget they are women. Cupid unblindfolded will cease to be Cupid and penitence will be the only lot for Psyche. This plea for sex taboos is, I surmise, the modern stand of those

---

the sense of "insult" based on resentment against the ruthless breaking down of one's social barriers? It may also be based, I suggest, on a still more primitive sense of defilement. The injury is actually conveyed through a kind of contagious magic.

* The tendency to live at second hand, through another, is a profound expression of sex, we are told, an impulse of passion. Accepting this analysis, is not the problem created for feminists far more baffling than any they have hitherto faced?

unwilling to forgo the protection of sex barriers. Far from wishing to let the natural differences of sex count in life, they seek to prescribe differences which may or may not correspond to fact, but which because they are arbitrary may be collectively and so comfortably encountered. In their great fear of sex they endeavour to make it a matter of collective habits, of dress, of manners, of occupations, of pastimes, particulars all subject to endless regulation. Is not so much regulation of a "mystery" suspicious? Were we less afraid of the real heterogeneities of sex, would we not be less insistent upon the differences we have provoked, those differences which are but blinds for the real differences? "This thing you may not think or do at all," says man to woman or woman to man, "because being different from me, your thought of it or your performance would be different and so disturbing. Take something else to think about or pursue, something not in my line. Keep out of my way as much as you can and I will keep out of yours. Whatever happens, let us not interfere with each other. Nothing else is quite as important to our comfort." Until comparatively lately this principle of non-interference has worked out well enough in economy*; in matters of passion it

* Perhaps because the economic differentiation of the sexes

has always been less of a success. Hence sex in its passionate manifestations has been subjected to endless regulation, regulation made rigid by the great fear of sex itself and complicated by all the other fears of unlike for unlike. Of this system of regulation we shall get the most comprehensive view through a consideration of marriage, ever society's mainstay in controlling the wayward-ness of sex, its vagrant and vehement impulses, its untoward and violent outbreaks, its blindness to the interests of others, its arrogances unsur-passed.

---

sets in at an early age, at a non-questioning, imitative time of life. When it starts later in life, as it tends to nowadays with us, it is more likely to be challenged. Similarly it is more likely to be questioned in business or in the professions than in more imitative pursuits like farming or housework.

XIII

MARRIAGE

MAKING a *mariage de convenance*, its embarrassments, and the distress incident to it are ever favourite themes of the playwrights. One of the plays of Terence, for example, opens with an account of a young man torn between love and duty, love for his mistress and duty towards the father bent on getting him married. "Pamphilus was in love with Bacchis here every bit as much as ever," narrates his slave, "when his father set about entreating him to marry, talking just the strain of all fathers."¹ Pamphilus dutifully marries his father's choice, but in another comedy of Terence the hero succeeds in disengaging himself from the lady chosen for him and in marrying, quite to his father's satisfaction however, his own true love. In this play, *The Lady of Andros*, it is the slave again who points out to you the situation. "So long as his years suited it," says Davus of his young master, another Pam-

philus, "he had a love-affair. . . . Now it's time
he took a wife, and to a wife he has turned his
thoughts."² Or, as we might say, having sown
his wild oats, the time had come for him to settle
down. Well it is if, like Pamphilus, a man can
marry his love, the Romans seemed to think,
and perhaps a marriage for love is a more secure
kind of marriage; but marry at any rate a man
should. To us this point of view is not unfamiliar,
but to many other peoples part of it at least is
entirely foreign. By them is made little or no
concession of personal choice in marriage. Marriages are planned arbitrarily by parents or kindred,
by the elders, by an overlord. It is their profit
or interest which is the determining factor, and in
making the match economic or political matters
or matters of family convenience or congeniality
are in question—girl-barter or bride-price or dowry,
alliance with other groups, the qualifications of
bride or bridegroom for fitting into the joint household or family connexion or for rendering it
personal services. Given such objects in marriage,
courtship naturally plays a minor part or no part
at all as a preliminary to mating. Matrimonial
go-betweens or marriage brokers or amateur
matchmakers negotiate its details; and in many
communities bride and bridegroom do not meet

before the wedding or even see each other. Allowed to meet, they may court each other only in set ways—by formal messages or declarations of regard, by exchange of prescribed presents, by stated visits, or by "keeping company" at appointed times or places.

Elopement is discountenanced and more or less penalized. So of course are misalliances, *i. e.* all marriages which violate the group rules of marriage or disregard the wishes of kindred. Breaking the ties of marriage is also penalized or made difficult. Divorce is upsetting to those who have arranged the marriage or to those who have come to associate two persons together in thought and in practice. It is because of the distress caused by disassociating persons presumed to be settled together once and for all, that opposition to divorce is even greater than opposition to marriage for love, and that freedom to marry is apt to be conceded long before freedom to divorce. A society's apprehensiveness about divorce is an expression of its fear of change and of its resulting desire that personality remain unvarying.

The better to preclude divorce and preserve the marriage ties, certain concessions, not to the demands of personality but to mere sex impulse, are wont to be made. Professional prostitution may be tolerated or encouraged as a protection to marriage, and even adultery at large, if it is covert, may be glossed over. A mistress is the more or less acknowledged complement to a wife, more rarely a *cicisbeo* to a husband.

Rebels against this double system of marriage and adultery there have been,—youths in New Britain who have escaped from under the coils of shell-money, thrown over their heads by relatives anxious to lassoo them, as it were, into an establishment,[3] Gotama and Jesus and their numerous imitators, Harold Godwin at the close of the eighteenth century, and no doubt many men and women of our own generation. But as a rule conjugality (with or without adultery) has been an acceptable system to the marrying as well as to their matchmakers. For the marrying too it has such obvious advantages—"some one now and then to yawn with,"* "the solace of a home," secure from "the torturing passions of intrigue."†

* As Byron, his mind on matrimony, wrote one day in his journal. (Mayne, i, 302.)

† In these terms Disraeli refers to the motives which prompted him to woo her who was to be Lady Beaconsfield. Besides, he adds, in words highly reminiscent of a Latin comedy, "my father had long wished me to marry; my settling in life was the implied . . . condition of a disposition of his property, which would have been convenient to me." (Moneypenny, W. F. *The Life of Benjamin Disraeli*, ii, 52. New York, 1912.)

Indeed conjugality may preclude the stress of courtship altogether, risks and strains due not only to group exactions or regulations, but to the nature of the relationship itself, subject as it is to doubts and uncertainties, indefinite, ever fluctuating. This unstable relationship is eliminated altogether, we noted, as a preliminary to marriage or so prescribed as to become, if desired, impersonal. Then courtship in marriage is of course rare—outside of certain very modern writers,* writers, too, who by their very suggestions seem to misunderstand the purport of marriage. For is not ease in satisfying the impulses of sex ever an essential to marriage? It is a provision at any rate most forms of marriage have in common. Exceptions are for the most part temporary. It is only on the night of his wedding that a Tipperah bridegroom has to steal into his bride's house and slip away before dawn.[4] Among the Albanian mountaineers a bridegroom takes his bride to his father's house, but he has to meet her in secret until she has a child.[5] Then again among many peoples conjugal intercourse during pregnancy, or the latter part of it, or during the period of lactation is taboo. But even this taboo is apt to be relieved for husbands through polygyny. Similarly polygyny

* Havelock Ellis, Ellen Key.

removes the restrictions upon conjugality professional travellers might\ suffer—traders, porters,
sailors, brigands.

To matrimonial ease privacy is a requisite, and
privacy—in physical relations—is ever guaranteed
the married. The doors of their apartments need
no bolts. Even lovers respect conjugal arrangements. The *ami de la famille* vows not to kiss
his mistress in her husband's house. Nor is a
mistress ever expected to be jealous of a wife.
The furtiveness of adultery is prompted not merely
by fear of punishment. It may be an expression
of conjugal consideration, quite sincere, however
at times unconvincing.

Unconvincing, unfortunately, for if the married
could really feel assured that their convenience
would never suffer, would there not be a great
diminution of matrimonial jealousy? Polygyny is
rarely complained of among frankly polygynous
peoples. A wife will often ask her husband to take
another,—a companion to lighten her burdens,—
or like Sarah or Leah she will herself give him a
handmaid. Similarly the polyandrous Thibetans
or the natives of Malabar do not mind sharing
their wife with a brother by blood or with a
brother Brahman. Nor do we hear anything of
complaining husbands among the Hassinyeh Arabs

who marry only for a stated part of the week,[6] or among those ancient polyandrous Arabs who visited their wives from time to time in the home of their father-in-law. The Massim or Blackfellow who refused his wife to her *eriam* or *piraungaru* and among many races the host who did not offer his to his guest would be considered a very churlish fellow indeed, one quite lacking in moral sense. But in polygamy the times and places of conjugal intercourse are apt to be regulated with care. The Caribs who married several sisters at one time lived a month with each in her separate hut. A Samoan gives each of his wives a round of three days.[7] A Moslem must visit each of his four legal wives in turn. So scrupulous was the native of Fûta, a Senegal kingdom, that when one of his wives lay in he spent the night appropriated to her alone in her apartment.[8] On marrying the same woman two Aleutian Islanders agreed together in advance upon the conditions on which to share her.[9] When an Arab left his staff outside his wife's door, a fellow-husband would not enter the room,[10] an effect less definitely produced by a cane in an Anglo-Saxon hall.

In Arabia a staff significantly placed is quite a sufficient guaranty of freedom from disturbance. Elsewhere marital monopoly has to be protected by measures more drastic or less symbolic, by harsh penalties for adultery, by the seclusion of wives, or where the extreme convenience of veil or zenana is unknown, by the unremitted or bellicose advertisement of marital proprietorship. Distinctive costuming, a distinctive headdress or haircut, a finger-ring or nose-ring, blackened teeth, a tattooed mouth, a title—wife of so-and-so or "the hissing 'missus' of too familiar husbands"—are all notices to intruders to keep away.

Men as well as women are advertised or advertise themselves directly or incidentally as married or unmarried—a fact still to be pointed out by the "hominist." Married Coreans wear a long outer robe which it is forbidden to wear before marriage.[11] They also put up the hair they had worn as bachelors in a queue into a conical mass upon their heads.[12] In Timor-laut a married man may never cut* his hair.[13] Masai bachelors have to be greeted by married women with "*Endakwenya,*" "O children!"[14] With us married men no longer wear wedding rings and to be indicated as the husband of your wife is a sign of derision, but if a man is married he is expected to let his acquaintances know it. Otherwise he is suspected of sinister purposes and in some covert way people feel

* Else his wife will die.

defrauded. Last summer I heard one of my Berk-
shire neighbours complaining that his coachman,
a married man, had spent several months with him
in the rôle of a bachelor, and about the same time
I learned that I was myself a target of criticism
because I had introduced to other neighbours an
acquaintance who had failed to at once proclaim
himself the *divorcé* he was. How he was to have
made known the fact, lacking a visible token,
whether it was deplored as in itself lessening his
matrimonial eligibility or whether the ground for
his divorce was merely disapproved of I did not
learn. He was divorced, the neighbours ascer-
tained, in New York, "and you know what that
means," they remarked.

We have already noted how well conjugal
monopoly may be guaranteed by magical or supernatural sanctions. That "infidelity" in husbands
is a ground for divorce in New York or in other
parts of the United States is usually acclaimed as
an outcome of Christianity—a little too confidently
maybe, in view of the lack of a like law in such a
Christian country as England. Then, too, monogamy is required of men—and far more strictly than
among us—among savages unmoved by Christian
doctrine, among the Andaman Islanders, the Veddas, the Igorot of Luzon, the Hill Dyaks of Borneo.

The existence of thoroughgoing monogamy among these peoples suggests, too, that just as the religious theory of marriage may have been exaggerated by the theologians, the proprietary theory may have been overworked by the ethnologists. I for one plead guilty. In discussions of prolonged widowhood and of widow immolation[15], so much was I impressed by the customs as expressions of property rights in women,* that I quite overlooked the very tenable theory that the customs were due to the feeling that the habits of a lifetime should not be broken up even by death. Prolonged widowerhood and husband immolation, infrequent as they are, must be explained on this theory.† Celibacy after an unsuccessful love affair

* The economic theory of widow immolation has been modified, if not transformed, by Lévy-Bruhl in accordance with his general theory of "participation." The widow together with the other property of the deceased are dispatched to him because they partake of him. They are a part of him. (*Les Fonctions Mentales dans les Sociétés Inférieures*, pp. 389-94.) Such an association, let me add, is too painful to the survivors to break up. The participation theory is a link between the property theory and the habit theory of widow immolation.

† Cp. *Religious Chastity*, pp. 4 n. 20, 22 n. 15, 74-5. Some of the practices characteristic of the weddings of the remarrying and much of the sentiment about them are also, I venture to suggest, an expression of perturbation caused by upsetting the "associations" of the living rather than of fear of encroaching upon the proprietary rights of the deceased. The *pat* marriages of India which take place at night, the widow-bride leaving her parents' house by the back door (*Ib.*, p. 289); Roman widow

is open to a like explanation, although there are more popular ways of explaining inability to fall in love again.

The economic analysis of marriage has undoubtedly obscured the psychological. To modern critics of marriage, marriage as a form of property holding was too enticingly open to attack for its proprietary features to escape exaggeration. Then too one is led astray by the proprietary terms of conjugal phraseology,* terms which on closer analysis are seen to express a man's dependence

---

marriages to which it was held indecent to invite many guests, and our own "quiet" weddings for widows are all no doubt in propitiation of the living rather than of the dead. In Albania and in the New Britain Islands we find indisputable evidence of the sensibilities of the living. If an Albanian widower remarries in what the relatives of the dead wife may consider indecent haste, they revenge themselves upon him by pouring water upon her grave in the belief that this libation will cause the second wife to be childless. (Garnett, *The Women of Turkey: The Jewish and Moslem Women*, p. 286.) At the wedding of a New Britain widower the kinswomen of his deceased wife go "on the loose," appropriating the weapons and dress of the men, painting red any man they can catch, and at a given signal falling upon the bridegroom's house and grounds and destroying everything in sight, their right to this so-called practice of *varagut* passing unchallenged. "The women are angry on account of the first wife," it is said. (Danks, p. 292.)

* In reading recently the semi-autobiographical histories of a class of Yale graduates, I was much struck by these seemingly proprietary terms. Wives are referred to as "good" or "the best a man ever had." "I couldn't get on without her," writes one man; "she puts up with all my ways," writes another.

on his wife for his psychical as well as for his
strictly material comfort and well-being. After
all is it not in love of the habitual rather than in
love of property that marriage is rooted? "The
selection of a particular hole to live in, of a particular mate, . . . a particular anything, in short,
out of a possible multitude, is a very wide-spread
tendency among animals," writes William James.[6]
"But each of these preferences carries with it an
insensibility to *other* opportunities and occasions—
an insensibility which can only be described phy-
siologically as an inhibition of new impulses by the
habit of old ones already formed. The possession
of homes and wives of our own makes us strangely
insensible to the charms of other people. . . .
The original impulse which got us homes, wives,
. . . seems to exhaust itself in its first achievements
and to leave no surplus energy for reacting on
new cases." Marriage is the indulgence of a
habit.*

The conception of woman as property greatly
facilitates of course this indulgence. Proprietorship enables you to have things just as you want
them, and to know where to find them. Proprietary marriage offers analogous conveniences. Be-

* "People have to get into the habit of being married." (*How
to be Happy though Married*, p. 104. New York, 1886.)

sides it thwarts intruders, classifying them, even
with conviction to themselves, as purloiners, and
it gets for marital proprietors the backing of other
ideas on the sanctity of property. It may also re-
inforce the sex feeling of subjection believed to be
natural to woman. Then too it is tempting to
treat a woman—or a man—as a chattel* rather
than as a personality; it disposes of her—or him—
with so little effort. It serves as a comfortable
stop-gap for a more exacting relationship. For
such reasons even relations outside of marriage are
apt to take on a proprietary character. Pericles
is said[17] to have kissed Aspasia as habitually as
the American husband who even kisses his wife
in the railway station. What fiercer demonstrations of conjugal proprietorship have ever been
seen than those sometimes incident to the "free
unions" of European cities, in such a union for
example as that described in *Les Hannetons?*
"You must not look at anybody's wife except your
neighbour's,—if you go to the next door but one,
you are scolded, and presumed to be perfidious,"
writes Lord Byron, weary of his rôle of *cicisbeo.*
"And then a *relazione* . . . seems to be a regular

---

* Or as a business partner. Economic reciprocity is as important an economic factor in marriage, let its critics admit, as
proprietorship.

affair of from five to fifteen years, at which period, if there occur a widowhood, it finishes by a *sposalizio;* and in the meantime it has so many rules of its own, that it is not much better. A man actually becomes a piece of female property."[18]

Since proprietorship is so effectual a barrier to a personal relationship, the very form of it in marriage is sometimes cherished assiduously, in the United States for example, even after the substance of it has passed away. Hence the representative character attaching to husbands in the old common law still figures in anti-suffrage argument. Hence, although the one flesh theory of Paulean theology is no longer preached upon seriously from the pulpit, the sentiment that a wife's place is by her husband's side is still effective in certain circles, the circle in which Mrs. Smith refers with pride to the fact that she has been never a night away from Mr. Smith since their marriage, or if from no choice of her own away, a day never passes without a letter to him, a spirit Mr. Smith may or may not thoroughly enjoy, although he usually shares in it through his own jocose references to his "better-half."*

* Is it because in one flesh no adaptations are necessary that this type of conjugal joke continues to be so reassuring and comforting? In general the conjugal joke owes its popularity, I

As mere conjugal barriers, these relics of the early church and of the English common law are not readily forgone. There are of course alternatives. A conjugal absence, for example, may be ignored. If a Fijian husband address the morning salutation he makes to others to his wife, she is likely to take it for a divorce.[19] No matter how long the Ainu husband has been away from home, he does not greet his wife on his return.[20] It is the practice of the Albanian wife to hide ceremonially when her travelsome husband goes and comes.[21] "After a long absence I have seen natives," writes Eyre of the Blackfellows, "never take the least notice of their wives, but sit down, and act, and look, as if they had never been out of the encampment; in fact, if anything, they are more taciturn and reserved than usual, and some little time elapses before they enter into conversation with freedom, or in their ordinary manner."[22]

Taking notice of a spouse at any time is apt to be discountenanced. Among the Andamanese remarks on his or her personal appearance or peculiarities are resented as indelicate.[23] A Mos-

---

fancy, to the satisfaction of feeling that your relation is impersonal, a relation of status, just as, if less humorous, you exclaim, "Isn't that just like a husband!" in order to indulge in the soothing feeling of being one of many.

quito Indian woman considers it improper to display emotion under any circumstances about her husband.[24] An Anglo-Saxon woman is supposed not to laugh at her husband's jokes or publicly applaud his speech. A Mandingo of Senegambia never jokes with his wives, deeming it incompatible with marital authority. If he laughed with them, a tribesman once explained, they would laugh at him.[25]

Then too intimate conjugal relations may be confined to set times and places. Spontaneity may go from them to such an extent that outside of a given room or a given forest, at a given hour, they are unthought of. In Fiji husbands and wives have to meet "from motives of delicacy" in the forest, a *rendezvous* kept in West Africa at the risk of slavery. There anyone discovering a couple making love out of doors could enslave them.[26] Among the Massim connexion never takes place indoors or at night but in the gardens and by day.[27] At Santa Marta, Colombia, the married also keep apart from each other at night,[28]—in the belief that a child conceived at night will be born blind.* In civilization too intimacy is apt to be localized

---

* Obviously an expression of sympathetic magic. Such an idea may suggest a habit or be itself suggested by habit. The outcome is the same—the stereotyping of a relationship.

or concentrated, as strictly perhaps in marriage as in prostitution.

By this concentration all the psychical activities of sex are naturally affected. Uncalled for, they flag and dwindle, and the relation between husband and wife becomes as unthrilled by the radiations of sex as if both were of the same sex. Under these circumstances they may have in fact less in common than if they were of the same sex, for the usual sex barriers may assert themselves, leaving each indifferent to many of the feelings or ideas of the other, arousing in both a reluctance or shyness about referring to certain topics* or a disinclination to listen to each other or even look at each other—a kind of conjugal deafness or myopia.†

Complete mutual obliviousness in getting used to each other is impracticable. Marriage like other set forms of social intercourse is expected to satisfy the instinct for companionship. Hence

* "Should a wife talk familiarly with her husband about religious matters?" asks Mrs. Graves in one of her *Twenty-five Letters to a Young Lady* (pp. 31–2. Chicago & New York, 1884). She should, answers the author quite positively, adding, "true, if he is an unbeliever, it may be distasteful."

† Such shortsightedness appears not to set in for three years of marriage among the Fûta, for not until that time has elapsed do wives permit their husbands to see them unveiled. (Astley, ii, 240.)

common interests in marriage are said to be most desirable—children, common acquaintances, a more or less common material equipment, the same household appointments, and, sometimes, even the same pursuits or pastimes. On the other hand childlessness, different friends, different tastes in expenditure, different "pleasures," absence, are all well recognized drawbacks to conjugality. To have nothing in common is a popular justification, if not a legal cause, for divorce. Whereas if you do things together, if you are interested in the same things, the need for divorce is not at all likely to arise, we are told.

But whether divorce occur or not, marriage appears to accomplish what is expected of it, only in some cases it is for a season, in others for a lifetime. Like other important social institutions it provides companionship immune to the influences of personality. Moreover it eliminates the extraordinary fears with which passionate contact with another personality is beset. It gives safety to passion, formalizing and limiting its demands. Then too it serves as a barrier not only against one person of the opposite sex but against a whole sex. By advertising the need of restricting the impulses of sex to a minimum it helps actually to restrict them. Moreover by fully satisfying those impulses of sex which most readily become a habit, the physical impulses, it curbs and dwarfs the impulses which are erratic and which are prone to upset habits, the habits of self and of others. Truly marriage is all its most ardent supporters believe. It is an incomparable protection to society—as society has been constituted.

XIV

IN THE FAMILY

A S the closest of relations between unlike persons and therefore the most to be apprehended, matrimony is of them all the most carefully regulated. But other relations between the unlike are also close enough in family life to arouse apprehension and suggest regulation. Perhaps the most general expression of this apprehension along the line of sex consists of incest rules. The forbidden degrees vary, covering, sometimes, as we have noted, a clan or a tribe; but the aversion to marriage with housemates is generally so marked, even when housemates belong to different clans, that it has been held that clan exogamy itself originated in this aversion.* The supporters of this housemate theory of exogamy generally point

* Westermarck, *Human Marriage*, pp. 324-31. Cp. Smith, p. 170. The division of the group into two exogamous moities and the subdivisions of these moities were provisions against the mating of brothers and sisters, parents and offspring, simple . . . incest rules. (Frazer, *Totemism and Exogamy*, i, 165.) The origin of the aversion to incest, Frazer adds, is a mystery.

out that novelty is a necessary sex stimulant.
"The newcomer filleth the eye."

It may be; but their exogamy theory rests, I
think, on an even deeper foundation. Is not
aversion to mating within both the clan and the
household due to the fact that novelty in customary relations is extremely disquieting, disquieting not only to the persons directly concerned,*
but to the groups to which they belong?

Incest, whatever its definition, is always a
matter of group concern and always subject to
punishment, heavy punishment too. If a New
Britain woman married within her class—as elsewhere in Melanesia the islanders are divided into
two marriage classes—her nearest kinsman would
seek her out and kill her the moment he found her.†
"The relatives of the woman would be so *ashamed*
that only her death could satisfy them."[1] In
Sumatra, Batak first cousins, a brother's son and
a sister's daughter, married each other at the risk

---

* "Disgust is associated with the idea of sexual intercourse
between persons who have lived in a long continued intimate
relationship from a period of life at which the action of desire is
naturally out of the question. This association cannot be
explained by the mere liking of novelty." (Westermarck,
Human Marriage, p. 353.)

† Her mate would be killed too. Twins of opposite sex are
killed. Belonging to the same marriage class, their embryonic
intimacy is improper. (Danks, p. 292.)

of being killed and eaten.[2] If persons of the same
name married in Yucatan they were ostracized,
in China, they were given sixty blows.[3]

On the other hand marriage outside of the
kinship group may also be opposed or penalized.
In south-east Australia, although the elders of
two tribes may sometimes for reasons of state plan
an intertribal marriage, there is always hot opposition within the tribe out of which the girl is to
marry.[4] An Athenian man or woman married
to an alien might be sold as a slave.[5] Did not
Miriam and Aaron speak against Moses because
of the Ethiopian woman he had married and were
not the Hittite wives of Esau "a grief of mind" to
Isaac and Rebekah? A proper young Hebrew
married his cousin. "Is there never a woman
of thy brethren, or among all thy people that thou
goest to take a wife of the uncircumcised Philis-
tines?" grumble Samson's parents and, subsequently Samson was thought no doubt by others,
if not by them, to deserve his fate.

Is not endogamy to be explained as an expression of the same aversion which is back of
exogamy*—aversion to a break in customary re-

---

* Westermarck holds that endogamous and exogamous instincts are alike (*Human Marriage*, p. 353), but in what way
alike he fails to state.

lations,* taking in endogamy the form of hostility
to the stranger? And may not the wide-spread
practice of avoidance among kindred be explained
on a like ground—dislike of a disturbance of habitual relations? "Avoidance" is most commonly
practised, as we might expect from our hypothesis,
by relatives by marriage. In some Victorian
tribes, for example, a woman's mother and aunts
may never in their lives speak to her suitor or
husband or even look at him. Nor may a man
mention his mother-in-law's name.[6] If a Wemba
see his mother-in-law coming along the path, he
must at once retreat into the bush. If he meet
her face to face he must keep his eyes fixed on the
ground[7]—a perfect picture for the modern car-
toonist.† A Zulu woman may have nothing to do
with her father-in-law or with any of her husband's
male relations in the ascending line. She may not
even name them to herself. She must to a certain
extent also *hlonipa*, to use the native term, her
mother-in-law.[8] A Beni-Amer woman is also
shunned, ceremonially, by her daughter-in-law.[9]

---

* The sporadic cases of uncle-niece, brother-sister marriage
have been explained and, properly I think, as due to economic or
dynastic reasons, to the desire to keep property or position in the
family.

† The mother-in-law joke is even staler than we sometimes
think.

On the Tully in Queensland a woman believes that her teeth would rot out were she to converse with her mother-in-law.[10] Among the North American Indians a man "avoids" his father-in-law as well as his mother-in-law.[11] So does a Fijian. Nor may a Fijian woman speak to her mother-in-law or her brother-in-law.[12] According to the *Lî Kî* a Chinese sister-in-law and brother-in-law "do not interchange inquiries about each other,"[13] a degree of avoidance we ourselves may practise almost as fully by the opposite method of "asking about" him or her as a form of respect.

The popular explanation of avoidance as an expression of respect comes nearer the truth, I fancy, than the orthodox scientific explanation of it as an incest rule.* For respectful conduct is merely treating a person in a way which puts him at his ease, which does not disturb his settled habits or rub him up the wrong way. Whereas to

* Parsons, Elsie Clews, "Avoidance," *The American Journal of Sociology*, January, 1914.

Tylor suggested that avoidance results from the intrusion of a person into a house in which he or she has no right and is therefore *cut*. ("On a Method of Investigating the Development of Institutions: Applied to Laws of Marriage and Descent," *J. A. I.*, xviii (1888–9), 247–8.) I differ with him merely on the point that avoidance is first a natural and then a ceremonious method of shirking an adjustment in a personal relationship, rather than a method of deliberately making a difference between the stranger and the family he or she marries into.

require any one to make a sudden personal adjustment is never good manners. Now it is noticeable that although avoidance may itself become a steadfast habit, in some cases after a lapse of time, after people have had a chance to accustom themselves to their new relation, shall we say, avoidance ceases. A Wemba may talk to his mother-in-law as soon as he is a father.[14] So may a Basuto and a Cree Indian, each after his marriage having had to be reticent. (A Cree's parents-in-law, we note incidentally, call him after his child, *i. e.* Father of so-and-so.*) Although an Armenian bride has to wear a veil of crimson wool over her face and is not allowed to address any senior member of her husband's household, in course of time the house-father, well assured of her behaviour, does remove her veil† and unloosen her tongue.[15]

* In accordance with his theory of avoidance, Tylor thought that teknonymy was a recognition of parenthood by relations by affinity. (*J. A. I.*, xviii, 248–50.) The birth of a child gave its parent a right in the house of its grandparents, maternal or paternal as might be. It does to be sure make him or her less of a stranger, but it also gives him or her a status, always easier to deal with than a personality. The Cree undoubtedly finds it less irksome to call his son-in-law by his status rather than by his personal name.

† He may not remove it for years and seldom does he remove it until the birth of a son. "A wife shows her character at the cradle," is an Armenian aphorism. Does it not express the feeling, howbeit rationalizing it, that a woman loses herself in her

But avoidance is practised not only between relatives by marriage. In the belief that the slightest contact will be followed by serious illness, at a certain stage in the Kurnai initiation the youths and the women are mutually taboo, [16] and what might be called avoidance symbolism figures in the initiation rites of several Australian tribes. In the Elema district, New Guinea, initiates leaving their *eravo* must not go near home to preclude all possibility of being recognized by their kinswomen. A mother who brings her son food must by some noise signal her approach to give him time to run back into the *eravo*. [17] We recall how the New Britain initiate has to hide away from his kinswomen at the risk of putting them to shame and forfeiting the property of his friends. Although a Hottentot boy was so tied to his mother's apron strings until his initiation that he was not allowed to talk with men at all, not even with his own father, after initiation—at eighteen—he had to avoid his mother altogether at the risk, if even he spoke to her, of being called a baby, [18] a trying experience to any boy.

---

child? Her baby diverts the attention of the family from herself and so makes her personality less fearsome. See Parsons, Elsie Clews, "Teknonymy," *The American Journal of Sociology*, March, 1914.

It seems to me that such furtiveness on the part of initiates is an expression of the sense of awkwardness felt on both sides, by boys and kinswomen alike, through the break in their habitual relations. It is also an expression of reluctance to enter into new relations with those one has associated with on other terms. In this case as in others the demand for an adjustment of personal relations is most easily met or dodged by the raising of fresh barriers.

Such barriers are put up quite often between brothers and sisters, sometimes between mothers and daughters, or between fathers and daughters. Fiji brothers and sisters may not speak together.[19] "You Whites show no respect to your sisters. You talk to them," a Crow Indian once said to Dr. Lowie.[20] In Queensland once a sister is grown up, her brother will not even mention her name.[21] Were a New Caledonian girl to run across her brother, she would have to throw herself on the ground face downward.[22] Were a Vedda girl to fall and hurt herself it is said that her brother could not give her a helping hand.[23] Among the Veddas a woman does not speak to her adult daughter, nor does a girl's father.[24] It would shock a Toda girl to be touched by her father.[25] I once asked an American father if he felt entirely at ease with his family of daughters. "We are on excellent terms," he rejoined. "They are very companionable; but of course there are things a man can't do with a daughter or talk over as he would with a son."

The Vedda taboo between mother and daughter betrays a desire for separation between those unlike in age. The difference in age between the members of a family is the second great source of unlikeness between them which has to be apprehended and regulated. It is dealt with in various ways. Children may live out. Among the Bontoc Igorot a child of two ceases to sleep at home. Boys go to the *pa-ba-fú-nan* or men's clubhouse, girls to the *olag*.[26] Bororo boys of Brazil go to the men's house as soon as they are weaned.[27] In New Guinea they go at four.[28] An Italian observer of England under Henry VII says that boys and girls at the age of seven or nine at the utmost are sent out by their parents, parents in every class of life, to live and serve in the houses of others, the parents in their turn taking into their service the children of others. "And on inquiring their reason for this severity, they answered that they did it in order that their children might learn better manners. But I for my part," adds their critic, "believe that they do it because they like to enjoy all their comforts themselves, and that they are better served by strangers than they would be by their own children. Besides which, the English being great epicures, and very avaricious by nature, indulge in the most delicate fare themselves and give their household the coarsest bread, and beer, and cold meat baked on Sunday, for the week . . . if they had their own children at home they would be obliged to give them the same food they made use of for themselves."[29] In later years in England the boarding school usurped the place of this domestic apprentice system. Boys were sent to school at seven or eight. "If any go at an earlier age," writes a pedagogue in 1612, "they are rather sent to the school to keepe them from troubling the house at home,* and from danger, and shrewd turnes, than for any great hope and desire their friends have that they should learne anything in effect."[30] Among ourselves we often say that it is time for John or Jim to go away to school to learn to be a gentleman, "not that he will learn much of anything else."

Even when children remain at home and when

* To keep them "out of mischief," as a modern writer puts it, "mischief meaning for the most part worrying the grown-ups." (Shaw, Bernard. *Parents and Children*, p. xl. New York, 1914.)

avoidance in its narrow meaning is not practised
between members of the family differing either in
age or in sex, reserves and constraints of various
kinds characterize family life. Often eating together "is not done." In the Society and in the
Sandwich Islands brothers and sisters, however
young, do not eat together. A son eats in company
with his mother only when he is at her breast.[31]
An Aeneze boy does not presume to eat at all
before his father. "Look at that boy," says the
scandal monger, "he satisfied his appetite in the
presence of his father."[32] Our children as a rule
eat their supper at least in the nursery. In
Kavirondo, in East Africa, father and sons never
eat together. Nor do brothers. The Kavirondo
women eat after the men,[33] a sequence common
in tribal or in peasant life.

When it does occur, the family meal has a
somewhat ceremonial character. It may be eaten
in silence or a need of unbroken talk may be felt.
The elders are usually served first. They are
entitled to certain portions and to the youngest
goes "the drumstick." The juniors may be expected to stand until their elders are seated. In
the Tonga Islands the juniors have to turn their
backs on the seniors.[34]

Shyness in the family is also expressed in the

quite common avoidance of personal names. An
islander of Torres Straits would be greatly mortified* were he to make a mistake and call a relative
by marriage by name.[35] Many peoples beside the
Crees are teknonymous. I have a Pueblo Indian
friend and several New England friends whose
wives always refer to them as the children's father.
Even as a *fiancée*, a Zulu woman is called mother
of so-and-so,[36] an anticipation which the American, however quick he is after he is a father to
call his wife "mother" or "mommer," might be
loath to make. In south-east Australia a man
speaks to or of his children as one counts on one's
fingers: *Tayling* or "Thumb" for the first-born,
Burbi or "First Finger" for the second child,
Youlgo or "Second Finger" for the third, etc.[37]
An Andamanese addresses his son as *dar ō dire*,
"He that has been begotten by me."[38] Everywhere offspring address their parents by their kinship term. It is contrary to Corean etiquette ever
to pronounce the name of a parent or of an uncle.[39]
The names of these relatives a Massim would
not only never think of pronouncing himself but
mention of them in his hearing he would resent
as insulting and cause enough for blows.[40] Senior
collateral relatives are addressed by their kinship

* See p. 94.

name both in the classificatory and in the lineal
system of kinship. In the classificatory system an
aunt is called "mother," an uncle, "father." In
the lineal system personal names for aunt and
uncle are sometimes used but never without the
prefix of the kinship term.* Not long ago senior
brothers and sisters and cousins were addressed
among us with a kinship prefix.

Is it far fetched to suggest that *avoidance* may
also be traced in family conversation or the lack
of it† both at the dinner table and away from it?
It has at times with us—unfortunately this is a
matter little observed outside of civilization—it
has such an unresponsive character that it has
been denied by some the name of conversation at
all. It is a kind of chatter made up of more or less
disconnected comments upon the neighbours or
the neighbourhood, upon the day's incidents or
accidents, upon "matters of general interest."
Feelings or points of view, ambitions or fancies

* "Why will you never call me 'Elsie' instead of 'Aunt Elsie'?"
I once asked a little nephew. "I don't like to," was for some time
his only answer. "It doesn't fit to call older people by their first
names," he added later. It is disrespectful to address elders by
name, say the Negritoes. (Read, W. A. *Negritoes of Zambales.*
Ethnological Survey Publications, vol. ii, pt. i, p. 56. Manila,
1904.) Boys are savages in more senses than one.

† "Avoid conversing in society with the members of your own
family." (Ward, p. 402.)

figure little if at all.   Then certain subjects without
which talk is likely in any circle to flag are never
referred to in the family—religion, sometimes
politics, sometimes arts or letters, almost always
sex.

The reluctance of parents in civilization to dis-
cuss with their children questions of sex* has
recently been remarked upon—dramatically and
even statistically.   Aware of the need of the discussion, an effort is being made to shift the responsibility from parents to school teachers.   Much
the same kind of shifting occurs, I surmise, among
savages.   Initiation ceremonies at which formal
education in sex is given are in the hands not of
parents but of the Elders or the medicine-men.
In the boarding-schools to which the youth of
West Africa are sent before initiation, instruction
in the duties of marriage and parenthood is given
by the old headmaster or mistress.

Among brothers and sisters too there is a tendency—where they talk together at all—not to
refer to sex topics.   A Blackfoot Indian has to be
careful in his conversation before his sisters "not
to offend their modesty."[41]   Among the Samoans

* Even impersonally.   As to personal experience, what father
would ever think of telling his daughter what he has really liked
in women, "what son ever dreams of asking his mother about
her marriage?"   (Shaw, p. xcvi.)

not the remotest reference to "anything, even by way of a joke, that conveyed the slightest indelicacy in thought or word or gesture" was ever made in the presence of brothers and sisters.[42] I am reminded of a reverend editor of the *Arabian Nights* who wrote that he had aimed to "purify" the text so that the "most innocently minded maiden" might read it aloud to her brothers and sisters "without scruple or compunction." Were Samoan maidens ever in the habit of rejecting a suitor, I wonder, by proposing to be a "sister" to him—a final way of stating that all references to sex were to be eliminated between them.

It must be said that with us jokes about sex are not altogether taboo—as inhibitory influences. Does not every prudent brother or sister conceal a love affair so as not to be "teased" about it? Teasing is the usual way taken by the family to show its members that references to any of their personal experiences except the most colourless are unwelcome in the family circle. In rare cases family banter or chaff may be disallowed—among the Omaha,* for example, if a son-in-law and mother-in-law or cousins of the opposite sex laugh

* Among the Sioux on the other hand joking with brothers- or sisters-in-law was in vogue. "To complain of such jokes or resent them, no matter how personal, would have been an unpardonable breach of etiquette." (Eastman, p. 268.)

at each other, the offender may be tickled or scratched or bitten⁴³ (without the right of reprisal)—but as a rule family ridicule is as effective as ridicule ever is to compel conformity and reticence.

But *avoidance* whether of kindred or of topics of conversation is not a sufficient barrier against intimacy or unwonted relations. Besides, companionship, if not intimacy, the home loving heart craves. Hence in family life as in marriage *set* forms of intercourse are desirable. The time for them or the occasion varies of course in different communities. Unknown in some places, the common meal is with us the most usual occasion for the family to come together. Not to eat with the rest of the family even when you are all away from home, travelling for example, would be considered unaccountable or selfish. Religious rites may bring the family together, whether the cult is of itself familial or merely encourages family prayers or going to church together. Family reunions in honour of birthdays or other anniversaries are in most families indispensable occurrences. They may be the only occasions when the family "connexion" is sure to foregather; although in most communities weddings and funerals are perhaps the occasions it is most certain to grace. These celebrations appear to be so ceremonial and so safely impersonal that even persons not on speaking terms with one another join in them. Family visits are also in order in connexion with all family crises, births, betrothals and marriages, deaths, and in token of respect from a junior to a senior member of the family. "I expect you to come and see me, you know I'm your aunt," says Aunt Sarah, or, "I'm the only aunt you have," she will add if she is, her insistence sharpened perhaps by the realization that with us aunts cannot absolutely count on receiving visits of ceremony.

Family meetings are characterized by stereotyped greetings and farewells. In Queensland when a mother and daughter have not met for a long time, the mother will rub a stick into the top of her head until it bleeds, crying and sobbing as hard as she can. When the daughter thinks her mother has sufficiently relieved her feelings, she takes the stick away.[44] In the Andaman Islands, relatives who meet each other after an absence throw their arms around each other's neck and sob as if their hearts would break until they are completely worn out.[45] If a Toda visits a village in which live female relatives younger than himself, he will be met by them, and greeted by the *Kalmelpudithti* or "leg up he puts" salutation.

Bowing down before him the kinswoman lifts to her forehead first one of his feet and then the other.[46] "Say good-bye," we bid Harry, as he starts to escape from the notice of a senior relative. "Will you not bless our children before you go?" says a Wemba to the elderly kinsman who visits him. The kinsman will then spit on the chest of each child and say, "May you keep well, my child."[47]

But even the meeting from day to day is formalized. A Chinese son is bound to pay his respects at dawn and "express his affection by the offer of pleasant delicacies." At sundown he "will pay his evening visit in the same way."[48] In the seventeenth century an English youth was told to crave his parents' blessing every morning and every evening on his knees.[49] Two generations back, writes Mrs. John Farrar in 1841, young persons rose and courtesied every time their father entered the room.[50] Nowadays, if they are mannerly they still rise at times for their mother, and rare is the good nurse who does not insist upon her charge kissing his mother good-morning and good-night.

Such demonstrations of affection are not the only impersonal expressions of family feeling. "Being companionable" may also be an attitude

of ceremony more or less preclusive, I infer, of a
personal relationship. I will give a few illustrations. In the Islands of Torres Straits, it is taken
for granted that a man's relative by marriage, his
imi, will go out with him in his canoe. In its bow
a special place is always assigned the *imi*, and it
is his business to hoist the sail, heave the anchor,
light the fire, and prepare the food.[51] In China
"after the proper dressing at cock-crow sons and
daughters-in-law should go to their parents and
parents-in-law. On getting to where they are,
with bated breath and gentle voice, they should
ask if their clothes are too warm or too cold, whether
they are ill or pained, or uncomfortable in any way;
and if they be so, they should proceed reverentially
to stroke and scratch the place. . . . In bringing
in the basin for them to wash . . . they will beg
to be allowed to pour out the water, and . . .
they will hand the towel. They will ask whether
they want anything, and then respectfully bring it.
All this they will do with an appearance of pleasure
to make their parents feel at ease."[52] With us the
joint family being less common than with the
Chinese, the ceremonial of being companionable
falls upon the unmarried offspring. A good son
will take some of his meals at home and now and
again spend the evening; a devoted daughter will go

driving with her father or mother or travelling or shopping or calling.* American brothers and sisters are less companionable; but a youth is generally expected to be his sister's escort. He feels more or less responsible for her, opposing in her "the slightest indecorum,"⁵³ and serving as a kind of watch dog. It is for him to protect her honour and the honour of the family. Elsewhere too this special function falls to brothers. "Last Friday when I came from work," said a Chukma to Lewin, "my father said to me, 'Where is your sister? She went out some time ago to fetch water and has not returned. I suspect she has run off at last with that worthless fellow Boopea, who is always hanging about the house.' On this I went and called two or three other young men who lived close by, and we went off after my sister. We met her and Boopea in the valley by the stream. Boopea was first in the path; my sister followed . . . holding his hand. Then I was enraged, and I ran at Boopea and cut at him with my dao; he leaped to one side and the blow fell on my sister. She said once 'Oh, brother!' and then fell dead."⁵⁴— Family "differences" do not always end so disastrously, but however distressing they may be,

* "A mother and daughter should call together." (*Manners and Social Usages*, p. 8.)

they appear to be less apprehended and less
guarded against than family intimacies, precluded
entirely as they are by avoidance or by conventional companionship, companionship at set times
and places, in set duties and responsibilities.*

* For these functions, as a whole, functions too elaborate and
comprehensive to be considered here, I must refer the reader to
general treatises on the family.

XV

AGE-CLASSES

WHERE birthdays are not celebrated or registration or enumeration blanks filled out,* it usually happens that age labels extend over comparatively long periods. Divisions of life history similar to those set forth so poetically by Jacques the misanthropical are followed very practically in tribal life. Upon them are based conditions of living, duties and obligations, restrictions and privileges. Everyone is expected to conform to the ways of his contemporaries and respect the different ways of his juniors or seniors. By this classification everyone may be treated not according to the needs of his personality, not according to his individual demands, but according to the prevailing conceptions about his age-

* Why is the recording of age so much insisted upon in these blanks? Is it merely for the purpose of identification as the rationalist asserts? And why is it bad manners in other situations to ask anyone his or her age? The joke about women not telling their age is like many another long standing joke quite worth ethnological analysis.

class, according to what as a member of that class he should be like. Age-classes are extraordinarily efficient barriers against personality.*

There is considerable variation in determining the boundaries of age-classes. Physical changes are taken into account—the signs of puberty, child-bearing, decrepitude; but it is usually ceremonial which definitely marks off one age-class from another, particularly initiation and marriage ceremonial. In spite of adolescence, where there has been no initiation, the class often remains unchanged. In Australia, in Fiji, in Samoa, and elsewhere an uninitiated man has to stay in the age-class of the boys.[1] Similarly unless a person is married,† he or she may have to stay in the age-class of the unmarried juveniles. Every unmarried Corean, for example, is treated as a child. Whatever his capers, he is never held to account, for he is not supposed to take life seriously. In social reunions he can take no part, and on affairs of importance he must hold his tongue[2]—a social position not very dissimilar from that at one time accorded Anglo-Saxon old maids.

* Their use to the primitive in meeting the changes he finds so trying I am analyzing in another study under the rubric of ceremonial reluctance.

† Initiation often affects marriage. Women will very commonly not marry uninitiated men.

Forms of address characterize different age-classes. Among the Koita of New Guinea, if an *erigabe*, a man in his prime, were speaking, he would address a man older than his father as *wahia;* a man of his father's generation as *raimu;* a man of his own generation as *vasi* or *biage;* a man of a younger generation as *roro.*[3]   Until a Kakhyen comes of age *Ma* is prefixed to his name, when of age, '*N;* but *Ma* is always used in addressing a junior, '*N* in addressing a senior.[4]   Among the Akikúyu a little girl is called *ka-re'-go*, a little boy, *ka'-he;* a big girl or boy not yet initiated or circumcised, *ki-re'-gu* or *ki'-he;* a girl or boy after initiation or circumcision, *moi-re'-tu* or *mu'-mo;* a woman betrothed or married, but not yet a mother, *mu-hi'-ki;* a warrior, *m'wa-na'-ke;* a married man *wa-ka-ny-u-ku;* a mother of young children, *wa-bai;* a married man with a child, *mun'-du mu-ge'-ma;* a mother of an initiated child, *mu-ti-mi'-a;* a man whose children are growing up, *ka-ra-bai';* a toothless old woman, *i-he'-ti;* an elderly man, *m'zur'-i*, one old enough to need a stick, *m'zur'-i a ki-a-na,* one extremely aged, *m'zur'-i a bou'-i.*[5]   Compared with these appellations, appellations no more particularized than those of most savages, how meagre our own terms seem—baby, master and miss, Mr. and Mrs.!

As for our elders, they lack special terms of address altogether, unless you count in the irregular practice of a man's saying "sir" to his senior.*

The habits of each age-class are rigidly regulated. Dieting according to age is very common. It is believed among the Kurnai that the breasts of girls eating kangaroo will not develop nor the beard or whiskers of boys eating quail or its eggs.[6] In New South Wales young men were told that if they ate emu they would break out in sores.† Nor could they eat duck. Only the married ate duck and only the old men, emu. Not until they were middle-aged could the Warramunga eat lizards, snakes, turkeys, bandicoot, emu, or echidna.[7] Kabuis youths are not allowed to eat cat,[8] nor Fijian initiates, river fish or eels or the

---

* By how many years it is rather indefinite. By fifteen, says one authority. (Harvey, p. 122.)

† In Queensland and Victoria boys and girls believe that if they eat forbidden food meteorites or lightning will kill them. (*Journal Anthropological Institute*, xiii, 1883-4, 294; *Proc. Linnæan Soc. New South Wales*, new ser., x, 1895, 393.) Several species of wild fowl and their eggs are supposed to cause the muscles of the boys of the lower Murray tribes to shrink and their hair to turn grey. (*Journal and Proceedings Roy. Soc. New South Wales*, xvii, 1883, 27.) Among the Wakelbura the spirit of forbidden game is thought to enter into its youthful eater, first causing him to utter its peculiar cry and then killing him. (Howitt, *Native Tribes*, p. 769.) Analogous magical phenomena are alleged to occur in our own nurseries. "If you eat so much cake, you won't grow up to be strong." "If you drink so much water, you'll turn into a brook."

best of the yams or vegetables.[9] Koita young folk may not eat certain varieties of fish lest their skin become harsh and unpleasant to the opposite sex. Among the Southern Massim none until past middle age may eat dog or turtle.[10] When an ox is killed among the Akikúyu,[11] the *N' jáma*, or the younger men, take the breast, the *Kiáma*, or men whose eldest child has been initiated, the belly and saddle, the *Moran'ja*, or men to whom a second child has been born, the back, and the youths, the head, neck, and ribs.* For Chinamen of fifty a finer grain was prepared, according to the *Lî Kî*, than for younger men. "For those of sixty, flesh was kept in store. For those of seventy, there was a second service of savoury meat. For those of eighty, there was a constant supply of delicacies. For those of ninety, food and drink were never out of their chambers. Wherever they wandered, it was required that savoury meat and drink should follow them."[12] Beef soup is reserved for the old men among the Sioux.[13] A Wagogo child may not eat the liver, kidneys, or heart of any animal.[14] It is only after initiation that a Yaunde may eat sheep or goat.[15] Only after we have "grown up," *i. e.* "come out," or gone to college, may we drink wine or take

* The women are allowed the inside.

after-dinner coffee. Beer we may drink sooner, at least in the form of shandy-gaff, but a Masai may not drink it at all until he is an elder.

While a Masai is a member of the warrior class, as he is sometimes for twenty years, he is in fact "in training," and he neither drinks nor smokes.[16] Among us the elders often extract a promise from their boys not to smoke until they are twenty-one. Formerly among the Sioux a young man could not use tobacco until he had achieved a record as a warrior[17]; in the Pueblo of Santa Clara not until he had killed a coyote.[18] When snuff-taking was in vogue with us, it was probably confined to "grown-ups." Among the Akikúyu it is to-day a habit only of the elders.[19]

Ornament and dress are almost invariably expected to be suitable to a given age. Among most savage tribes children go clothesless until adolescence. At this time our girls lengthen their skirts and wear stockings in bathing. At fifteen a Persian boy is given his ceremonial girdle.[20] Only after initiation could a Queensland youth wear the grass-necklace, the human-hair waist-belt, and the opossum-string phallocrypt of a man.[21] At a corresponding age our boys pass from short trousers into long, and a little later acquire "evening clothes." On March 16, in his fifteenth or sixteenth year, a Roman boy puts on the *toga virilis*.[22]

Halamahera boys in the Moluccas may wear no red * in their clothes before they are made men.[23] The head kerchief of Aeneze girls is red, of their seniors, black.[24] In China violet and black are worn only by old ladies.[25] We ourselves do not like to see a girl wearing black, and a generation ago old ladies were supposed not to wear anything else—except perhaps grey or at a stretch pale lavender. Fond of pink, they might wear it only surreptitiously. "I always run in plenty of pink ribbon in my things, and I have pink ribbon garters!" confesses one old lady who has had to forgo her favorite colour—on the outside.[26]

Textures as well as colours are proper to different ages. The veil of the Venetian maiden was of

---

* Given colours are appropriate not only to age-classes and to royalty. There is white for ghosts (white is a sacred colour too among the Ainu.—Batchelor, p. 20); black and white and mauve for their mourners (yellow in China); black and red for demons; blue for the Virgin Mary—and ultramarine at that when her worshippers can afford it. There is the yellow novel, the red-covered guide book, the black bound Bible. Almost every group associates itself with a colour—schools, castes, nations. (Once in Turkey no foreigner was allowed to wear green, Mahomet's colour.—*A Pepys of Mogul India*, p. 5. New York, 1913.) The sexes have their own colours, beginning in the nursery with blue for boys, pink for girls. Then there is the taboo on many colours for men, a taboo very modern and very rigid.

silk, of the Venetian matron of holland, edged
with bone lace.[27] Velvet is not suitable for a
girl, we say, nor dimity for a matron, and is not
a soft lace the most becoming thing an old lady
can wear? At seventy a Chinaman "does not
feel warm unless he wears silk."[28] Nor may
a Chinese boy wear fur.[29] Sixteenth-century
Italians criticised a young man who wore fur.[30]

Not until a Kikúyu woman's first-born is
initiated does she wear copper earrings.[31] Between initiation and marriage Kikúyu maidens
wear on their forehead a band of beads and shell
disks,[32] just as our own young ladies when they
"come out" may wear a necklace of pearls, small
pearls—perhaps seed or fresh-water pearls, at
any rate not large pearls—for costly jewelry is in
bad taste for a girl. Her first handsome piece
of jewelry is probably a wedding gift, although
our practice is not as uniform in this matter as the
Kikúyu. The Kikúyu bride regularly receives
from her father the iron collar which befits a
matron.[33]

Mating is regulated according to age. In most
savage tribes initiation rites take place at adolescence and as a rule marriage is prescribed at a
more or less set period after initiation. By
societies whose method of time keeping has ad-

vanced, it may be prescribed at a set age.   But
in either case failure to mate at the customary
time is derided or penalized.   In the Islands of
Torres Straits a youth whose beard begins to
get heavy or a maiden whose figure is maturing
is ridiculed into marriage.[34]   In East Central
Africa a girl learns that unless she marries as soon
as she is nubile she will die.[35]   At twenty the
Jewish youth was "numbered" and unless he
straightway married he was outcasted as a criminal.
Unmarried Romans between the ages of twenty
and fifty for women, of twenty and sixty for men,
were subject to tax, they could not become heirs
except to near relatives, and they could not receive
legacies.[36]   After sixty marriage evidently was
not to be expected among the Romans.   Among
us the marriage of an elderly man or woman is
apt to be a little ridiculed.*   Love making by the
old† is sure to be.   "It were no meete matter,
but an yll sight to see a man—being olde, hore-

---

* The birth of a child, at least of a first child, to those getting
on in years also seems to us a little ridiculous.   In the Western
Islands of Torres Straits the child of such a couple was invariably
killed, so much did its parents dread the ridicule and talk its
birth occasioned.   (*R. C. A. E. T. S.*, vi, 109.)

† But "people remain much longer in the sexual arena" than
formerly.   "A bishop's wife at fifty has more the air of a *femme
galante* than an actress had at thirty-five in her grandmother's
time."   (*Shaw*, p. xcviii.)

headed and toothlesse, full of wrinckles, with a lute in his armes playing upon it and singing in the middes of a company of women, although he coulde doe it reasonablye well. And that, because suche songes conteine in them wordes of love, and in olde men love is a thing to bee jested at."[37]

About love making by their juniors, however, the old have much to say. They are very apt to make the match or at least to pass on it. They give instruction too on sex habits in general, and violation of their rules they usually penalize. The code they lay down for their juniors is apt to differ from their own. At the corrobborees of the Narran-ga, the old men took at pleasure any of the young wives of the class they had a right to marry into, whereas if a young man wanted such a loan he had to give his own wife in exchange.[38] Among the Dieri only the older men, they who have passed through the Mindari ceremony, have the right of *piraru* or group marriage.[39] It is customary for a M'kikúyu not to add to his three wives until his first-born child is taken into the tribe.[40] Even when there is no formal limitation for the younger men, the Elders are often the only men rich enough to be unhampered polygynists or polygynists at all. Sometimes indeed the juniors cannot afford even one wife; they may be without enough to marry on at all, having to live in poverty-stricken celibacy, poor old bachelors. Under such circumstances the theory of not coveting your neighbour's wife becomes of course very important—to the peace of the Elders. To ensure it, they find that it is well to separate the youths more or less from the women—sometimes for months, sometimes for years—and to impress upon them, particularly at initiation, when the youths are most under their thumb, the impropriety of interfering with other men's women, let alone its disastrous consequences, juridical and supernatural.

The Elders are able to attach a supernatural sanction to marriage as well as to any other custom they may cherish because supernaturalism has ever been largely under their control. They are the heads of totemic cults, of secret societies, of religious hierarchies. From these organizations the young are wholly excluded or admitted to a membership more or less restricted. Ohiyesa, *alias* Charles A. Eastman, a Sioux, writes that his grandmother told him that were the medicinemen to discover him and the other little boys playing "medicine dance," they would shrivel up their limbs with slow disease.[41] The young have little to do at any rate with the gods or their

proxies. Once when because of his wrong diag-
nosis a Wagogo medicine-man was ridiculed by
the friends of his patient, an adult woman, he
told them that they were *too young* to have con-
sulted him.[42] If a Caffre child have an ominous
dream, he tells his mother and she intercedes for
him with the appropriate spirits.[43] "Suffer little
children to come unto me" is far from being a
wide-spread dictate among the gods.

In all ancestral cults it is the oldest member
or members of the family who are responsible to
the family ghosts. Food for the ghosts of the
Islands of Torres Straits is collected and spread
out for them only by the old men.[44] "It is a
strange notion which prevails in the world, that
religion only belongs to the old," writes Hannah
More,[45] more perplexed than she would have been
had she known more about the Islands of Torres
Straits. But even in her own island the clergy
are no longer young when they hold high office.
Then too preferment in the Church of England as
in any hierarchy is optional with the elders. It is
too in secret societies whose membership is selec-
tive.[46] Even in Australia where as a rule every
youth may pass through every stage of initiation,
among the Dieri only a certain number of youths
are picked, *and they are picked by the Elders*, for the

rite of *kulpi* or sub-incision which qualifies them to hold the important positions of the tribe—to be the tribal emissaries, the leading dancers at the corrobborees, and in time members of the "great council."[47] What attributes in the Dieri youths influence the Elders in their selection we are not told, but among them are no doubt the very traits which lead older men among ourselves to give positions in business or in the professions to young men of promise—a modest and respectful bearing, ingratiating ways with older people, conformity in general to the standards set youth by age.

Membership in the Dieri council is not only determined by the original selection of the Elders; the candidates themselves have to be of an advanced age. Statecraft like supernaturalism is ever largely in the hands of the Elders. Very primitive societies like the Australian are indeed absolute gerontocracies. Their only government is a council of the Elders. At their meetings no young man* may speak.[48] Even under chief-

* Nor is their opinion ever to any extent considered. In Victoria, for example, they are under no circumstances allowed part in so important a matter as planning for intertribal visits. (Smyth, i, 133.)

"Put not yong men in authority that are to prowde and lyght," (Furnivall, p. 95) is a line that undoubtedly expresses the Black-fellow as well as the early English point of view.

tancy or monarchy a council of the elder statesmen or senators is influential. Membership in the government of a democracy may also be conditioned by age. None is eligible to the Senate of the United States under thirty or to the Supreme Court or the Presidency under thirty-five. In the Soudanese democracy of Wadai although young men may be present at the council, they have little influence and seldom speak.[49] Like well trained children they are seen but not heard.

But outside of council meetings speech is standardized by age. According to the *Li Ki* no well-bred Chinaman will introduce in conversation, "irregularly" is the word, a subject on which his senior has not touched. And it is contrary to his sense of propriety when his elder asks a question not to answer it, although belittling at the same time his ability.[50] In few savage tribes will a young man express an opinion before his elders, if he expresses it at all, without much caution and a show of diffidence. Among the Sioux he does not speak at all unless he is spoken to.[51] "You would not talk of your pleasures to men of a certain age," writes Lord Chesterfield,[52] a "mark of deference and regard" youth still pays to age, even if age has begun to question it. "Just as I have weeded my talk a hundred times out of respect to the young, these dear children weed their talk from respect to the old," writes a modern old lady in a vehement protest against being talked at or for whenever she joins a circle of polite young people.[53] This particular old lady does not refer, like most old people, to a dislike for current slang —she is perhaps too young to feel it. But such verbal novelties are apt to be spared the ears of seniors. Children on the other hand are often told not to use "grown up" words. "You talk like your grandfather," or "like a little old woman," is said in ridicule to a "precocious" boy or girl. "Lie" is generally held to be a word unbecoming to a child's mouth; "fib" is a better word for them to use. Similarly for many other simple acts or objects there are nursery paraphrases.

Besides the expurgation of vocabularies or of topics of conversation, there are many other particulars of behaviour age determines. In Victoria in visiting a camp the oldest man of the company walks first, the younger men following.[54] The Kikúyu warrior for whom the girls stand aside, himself stands aside for old women.[55] A Masai warrior dare not greet an elder until the elder has greeted him.[56] "In meeting your elderly friends in the street," counsels the *Young*

Lady's Friend,[57] "look at them enough to give them the opportunity of recognizing you; and if they do so, return their salutation respectfully, not with the familiar nod you would give to one of your own age."—"Never lounge on a sofa or rocking-chair," the early Victorian continues, "whilst there are those in the room whose years give them a better claim to that sort of indulgence." Mabuiag lads are instructed not to stand upright in the presence of the old men.[58] Among the Mpongwe the young may never approach the old or even pass their huts without crouching with head bared. They may not sit down near them nor hand them anything without dropping on one knee.[59] The Chinaman has to carry a stool and a staff for the use of his elder. When following him he must keep his head turned in the same direction the elder is looking.[60] The Hebrew was taught "to rise up before the hoary head," and we teach our children to stand when their elders enter the room.

> " Loke, my son, that thow not sytte
> Tylle the ruler of the hous the bydde."[61]

At the table our elders are always served first. In China until an elder has emptied his cup, a junior "does not presume to drink his."[62] Under

no circumstances may a Wemba ask his senior
for a smoke. All he can do is to sit down near
the older man and look wistful.[63] Nor does a
Corean[64] or a Pueblo Indian* smoke before his
father.

In graver ways too "grey hairs" have to be
considered. They are a protection against the
vehemence of youth. Once during a general row
in a group of Blackfellows, Spencer and Gillen
saw one of the younger men, *i.e.* a man between
thirty-five and forty, a medicine-man too, try to
shake one of the older men. At once, at this
serious offence, his precious medicine powers left
him.[65] Assault of an elder is hateful to the gods,
opines Plato in urging that seniors by twenty
years never be molested—"out of reverence to the
gods who preside over birth."[66] This platonic ad-
monition is lived up to very practically by the
Bushongo of the Congo. A Bushongo elder has
only to put his stick across the doorway of a hut to
close it against intruders[67] and protect himself, if
need be, against his juniors.

Classification by age serves not only as a barrier
between persons of different age; it provides or

---

* Unless his father has become "Americanized." Moreover
to American cigarettes the rule appears at times, I have noticed,
not to apply.

enforces companionship between those of the same age. Among the Koita a very close relationship called *henamo* is formed between boys* born on the same day or, where the definition has been stretched, about the same time, their fathers having exchanged presents at their birth. [68] Among the Kurnai all the lads who have gone through the Jerail initiation rites at the same time are accounted brothers. Married, each addresses the wives and offspring of the others as "wife" and "child." [69] In South Africa the contemporaries of the son of a chief are circumcised together with him at puberty, and all become his lifelong companions. Their brotherhood takes his name. Members of Bechuana brotherhoods are supposed never to give evidence against one another and always to share their food with one another. [70] With us ties between classmates are not as lasting or as close, although boys are sent to school or college primarily very often to learn "how to get on with other boys." Periodic class reunions, however, are ceremonially maintained; many men are able to cherish classmate sentiment for a fellow without having any other interest in him

* Girls may become *henamo* in the same way as boys; but the relationship is by no means as serious. It is often allowed to drop when one of the girls marries. Girls, it is said, are no good for *henamo*.

13

whatsoever, and it is generally considered more difficult to refuse a money loan to a classmate than to another.

In Uripiv, there are ten age-classes and every male has to mess with his own.[71]   Among the Makalaka, north of the Zambesi, the tribal elders eat together.   So do the young men and the boys.[72] Married people among the Andamanese give dinners to which girls* and young men are not invited.[73]   At our dinner parties, even when they are invited, they may be expected to keep more or less to themselves.   The girls have "jokes and stories in a corner by themselves, whilst the matrons discourse of their own affairs. . . . Presently . . . the gentlemen come dropping in, the young ones first and the politicians last."[74] At women's lunch parties girls and matrons are still more segregated.   "What is the girl like?" a while ago I asked a woman who had been visiting a mutual acquaintance, the mother of a *débutante*.   "I don't really know.   I hardly ever saw her," was the answer.   "She had so many engagements she did not lunch with us once during my visit."

On many occasions besides feasting or the daily meal age-classes keep together.   The Uripiv

* See p. 113 for the Japanese custom.

age-classes sleep as well as eat together.   In a
Masai kraal the huts are grouped together according to the age of their tenants, and away
from home a tribesman must seek for hospitality
among the huts of those of his own age.   He is
never denied, because a Masai fears were he
churlish he would be cursed by his age-class and
die.[75] Among the Massim at Bartle Bay the
members of the same *kimta** also show one
another hospitality.   The women of the same
kimta go fishing together; the men hunt together
and co-operate in irrigation work.   The old men of
the Massim have their own *potuma* or club house,[76]
and in some of our club houses there are, I am
told, old men's corners.   "Just as I see my son
serving the friends of his own age and allied with
him in his affairs," remarks an elderly Roman, in
one of the plays of Terence, "so it's right we old
fellows should gratify other old fellows."[77]   The
Zulus of Angoni go to war in companies divided
by age.[78]   The military conscription of Europe is
based on age.   Dancing as well as campaigning
may be affected by age.   Until recently† in the
United States at dances for young people the
matrons sat apart, sometimes in seats especially

---

* Age-class of children born in every period of about two years.
† Before the introduction of "turkey trotting."

assigned to them, it being "undignified" at their age to dance. The Kikúyu matron does not go to dances even to look on. Her husband takes part in them as long as he has only one child; but she gives them up as soon as she is married. [79]

Is it not apparent how much well-defined age-classes simplify life—at least from the primitive point of view—and why any tampering with their boundaries like that attributed to Dr. Osler, for example, or like the recent changes in the age limits for federal labourers and federal judges can be so disturbing and arouse so much criticism? Upsetting as such changes may be, they are, however, nothing like as distressing as doing away with age-classes altogether. "All the men and women in Paris are of uncertain years!" exclaims Zeyneb Hanoum, [80] her dismay and resentment unconcealed. Although in kindly moments we may describe a woman as not showing her age or as being the age she looks, when we feel less complimentary do we too not refer to her more or less derisively as of an uncertain age?

XVI

CONCERNING GHOSTS AND GODS

WE have noted primitive man's desire to run away from or to exorcise his ghosts. Rarely does he show any desire for intimacy with them. This does not mean of course that relations with them are supposed to cease. Their aid is sought, their anger deplored, their malice outwitted. They hang about, it is thought, to be appeased, placated, flattered. But all such relations are readily depersonalized. Funeral and mourning practices are ever highly conventional. In the first place because, death being as we say a shock, a round of ceremonies disguises or at least postpones the necessity of readjustment both for the mourners themselves and for those who would otherwise be disturbed by the mourners' state of mind. But in the second place because formal manners are the easiest way of showing the dead as well as the living their place.

Funeral and mourning practices would of themselves keep the dead at a distance since they make communication with the living difficult,* but ghosts are also given to understand explicitly that they may communicate with the living only at set times or places and often only through appointed persons. Ghosts are generally expected not to walk, not to wander from the locality of their grave or shrine; but there to receive the ceremonial visits of their friends and accept their attentions. A ghost who haunts a place to which he has not been invited runs the risk of being shown quite pointedly that he is intruding. Then a ghost may be expected to be "at home" only at set times—at midnight, on the anniversary of his death or on the day of the week—the *arpatzuol*, the Todas call it,¹—at the *anthesteria*, on All Soul's night, at death feasts. His resurrection may even be postponed to as indefinite a time as the "sounding of the last trump." At death or memorial feasts ghosts have to appear, when they appear

---

* Whatever may be the reason for wearing crêpe veils or clothes of special cut or colour, the pipeclay the mourning Blackfellow smears on ᵼhis body or the chaplet of bones his widow hangs over her face look very much like disguises from the ghost. Taboos against naming the dead or unwillingness to talk about them except in the past tense take their absence, to say the least, for granted. When alms are given or prayers said for them to shorten their stay in purgatory, their banishment from our circle is certainly not left in doubt.

at all, in the person of appointed representatives. They themselves have no choice. At other times representatives, *i. e.* mouthpieces or mediums are also selected for them, sometimes their widow, actual or ceremonial,² sometimes the head of their family group, sometimes the priest in ordinary.

Gods, whether nature spirits or ghosts particularly distinguished or long-remembered, have more freedom than the average ghost. But boundaries are set for them too, sometimes a lake or a mountain peak, sometimes an image or a temple, sometimes a given bodily function or disease, sometimes merely the boundaries of science. The Haytians told Peter Martyr that one of their gods was such a rover that they had to chain him down in a room at the top of their chief's house.³ Omnipresence is an attribute few gods indeed are possessed of. Gods too are usually in charge of special persons who act as their go-between with the public. The keeping of private spirits is generally discouraged*— sometimes mildly as in the excommunication of Christian Gnostic, Pietist, or Protestant, some-

---

* There are of course exceptions. One of the functions of the Gold Coast medicine-man is to make a personal fetish for applicants. The Tonga Islander has a tutelar god, the Catholic a patron saint, the Jew a good angel and a bad, and the North American Indian a *manitou*.

times more violently as in the burning or drowning of the medieval witch over-familiar with Satan or one of his minions. Again like ghosts gods are kept in their place through ceremonial. They have to receive visits and accept presents quite as formally as royalty. The compliments paid to them are set too, for divine attributes and powers are unchanging. Representing as they do a specific quality or force, the favours asked of them are naturally always of the same order. Steadfast in their functions, the gods are credited too with steadfast views or convictions. They are invariably conservatives. They may be given the privilege of an occasional change of heart or of temper, but their mind they may not change. Hence conformity with their unvarying opinions is judged pleasing to them and they are expected to feel aggrieved or dishonoured by non-conformity. Their habits being fixed, they are highly susceptible to insult and they have a very nice sense of the honour due them.

Many other human traits besides the desire to be imitated or agreed with or considered are ascribed, we know, to the gods. The more they resemble their worshippers, the more sympathetic and accessible they appear. Hence even nature or animal gods are likely to become anthropomorphous, and gods of all kinds tend to be assimilated in one way or another with their priests. But because of this very humanizing of the gods there is always a certain amount of danger in dealing with them. They may be superhumanly conservative, but their temper is human enough to be uncertain. Tact and resourcefulness are required of their mouthpieces or managers.

In all but effete cults priestcraft is indeed an exacting pursuit, and one none too safe. Priests have had to take chances. There are the gods themselves, fickle, if conservative, and then there are their worshippers, exacting if not critical. Failure to forestall events or in emergencies to turn the heart of the god readily embroils a priest with his people. In times of tempest or flood or drought,* of famine or blight, of sickness or epidemic, of war, the priest may be held responsible. It is easy for him to be discredited and to fall into disrepute. Then, too, whenever he is suspected of practising black magic, he naturally makes bitter enemies.

It may take not only courage to be a priest, but in primitive society a spirit of adventure. A medicine-man, as we have noted, is usually an explorer

* Weather doctoring is particularly hazardous. The rain makers for the tribe, Soudanese chiefs lose their position, for example, when they lose their skill. (Wilson and Felkin, i, 82.)

of more than one world, besides being an adept in reincarnating himself in other creatures, animal or human. But more than this, he has to have the hardiness to stand alone and to be more or less shunned by his fellows. In the first place, isolation, he knows, is necessary to his prestige. In the second place, he betakes too much of the nature of his god, his people feel, for ordinary, comfortable social intercourse, and so they willingly "observe the dignity of his cloth." It is not to every social gathering among us a minister is invited and to avoid the bad luck of meeting his priest on the road a Russian peasant, it is said, will go considerably out of his way.

Given a gregarious life, courage to stand being left alone undoubtedly gives a priest prestige, but after all it is his taking of responsibility which gives him his great hold on primitive society. Through his own initiative with deity he enables the layman to have a sense of being on good terms with the gods without having to enter into close and so trying relations with them. In other words the priest is an expert—the first expert indeed. From him all our other social experts have been differentiated.*　But however diverse

* To become his rivals. The clerical hold weakens with the social recognition of every new kind of secular expert. May not

their enterprises, their value to society is fundamentally the same as his. They all relieve the average man of the necessity of thinking for himself, of being bothered, of making new adjustments, of breaking down his habits. All he has to do in a trying place is to take the advice of the expert, *i.e.* satisfy his old instinct of imitation.

In the contrivances of the supernatural expert much of the social character we have been studying is seen at its plainest. Dealing only with imaginary beings, priestcraft has been unchecked in carrying out the collective conceptions of society. In priestcraft the play of collective theory has been unthwarted by iconoclastic rebels and unmoved by physical conditions.* It has succeeded in modelling the gods as men would, if they could, model themselves. Man has not made his gods in his own image but in the image he would see of himself, unchanging beings, with set characteristics, with set interests in a stable *milieu*, with habits undisturbed, devoid of personality. The appeal to such beings is simple and manifest. One can always know what will interest them and how they stand.

---

irreligion be defined as the following of lay leaders or as dependence upon the pragmatic in place of the religious ecologist?

* We have here, I think, an explanation of the conservatism of the churches, of the conservative nature of religion.

XVII

AN UNCONVENTIONAL SOCIETY

IT appears then that Society is the compromise it is always said to be,—a compromise to gratify naturally inconsistent inclinations, the instinct of gregariousness and the instinct for routine.* Companionship it supplies, but only the kind of companionship warranted not to derange habits or influence personality. Against the psychical changes naturally resulting from personal contacts society sets its face. Its means are simple. It raises up barriers between the unlike, restricting companionship to those it accounts alike, to those of the same age or sex, of the same calling, of the same house, tribe, caste, or country. Individual variations within the group it ignores or persecutes.

* When the routine of the individual is just the same as his group's, it is of course not incompatible with the completest kind of gregariousness. It might well be held indeed that the instinct for routine was an outcome in part at least of the gregarious instinct, that of our own accord we do nothing "differently" because others do not, that we do as others do the better to be with them.

From the remotest times homogeneous groups
have been numerically increasing, but it was
only the other day, comparatively speaking, that
the barriers between the heterogeneous, between
those unlike in status, were ever called into question.   The conception of personality distinct from
status is also recent.   Conception and arraignment
spell social revolution on a great scale, for do they
not mean that dread of change is no longer the
controlling social factor it was?

How has this momentous change itself come
about?   Largely, it seems to me, through the
passing of social control into younger hands; and
youth is less averse than age to change.   Thanks
to modern economy, persons of leisure, the only
persons free to direct social adaptations, are no
longer almost certain to be old.   Younger men
and women* recruit the leisure class.   There is
also more leisure in the lives of all younger persons
and therefore more opportunity for them all for
self-direction in social relations.   They have begun to slip from under the yoke of their elders.

Gerontocracy has had a grave blow too in the
decay of supernaturalism.   Ghost cults necessarily

* Outside of our culture, of course, younger women have
recruited the leisure class, but they have been too ignorant
comparatively, or too exhausted by child-bearing, or too bound
by caste restrictions, to count as social leaders.

give prestige to those on the verge of becoming
ghosts themselves.   Then the deceased Elders,
bound by the sense of their age-class, or in well-
developed ancestor worship by their recognition
of family succession, are always expected to back
up their living contemporaries or successors.   In
still other ways the authority of the old has
been affected by the passing of supernaturalism.
Supernaturalism depended much on tradition
—after as well as before the use of writing—and
as the memories of the old were the depositories
of tradition the Elders always commandeered
important places in all magical or religious systems.   Through these systems early society is
largely controlled.   Upon them depend, people
think, plant and animal reproduction, birth and
death and health, success in hunting, in fighting,
in adventuring of any kind.   But the time comes
when supernaturalism has to relinquish its claims
to control nature and through nature society,
and then the magical or religious parts once so
potently filled by the old become intrinsically
insignificant.   Whenever a totemic practice is
discredited or a nature cult or one of the historical religions, the hold of the Elders on society is
weakened.

Undermining the influence of the Elders is one

of the many indirect ways in which science* has
ever made for social change.   As soon as science
is called upon to effect social changes directly,
the status of the Elders will be even more radi-
cally affected.   Much of the routine of life will
still be in the hands of the old, as much of it as
possible in fact will be turned over to them, they
liking it and being fitted for it, but no prestige
or authority will attach to them, nor will their
work or functions be accounted superior.   In
many respects the old will be better off than they
were, but "honour and respect" will no longer be
a due to grey hairs *qua* grey hairs.   Then as the
only status the old may set up a claim to will be
one of inferiority, their age-class will tend to disappear.   And has it not in fact already begun to
disappear?

This "placing" of the Elders, their re-valuation
or elimination as a class, will of course in turn
accelerate social change.   A far greater accelera-
tion will be due to the frank determination by
scientists and by mere pragmatists alike to give
to social facts the same consideration they give
to the facts of nature.   The determination once
reached and the idea made a commonplace that

*Or, as Lévy-Bruhl would say, the increase of concepts at the
expense of mystical, prelogical representations.

society may control changes in itself through knowledge, individual failure to change with society will be accounted cowardice, clinging to the habitual, immorality, and the conservative, not the progressive, will be ever on the defensive.* Very quickly then will the social barriers we have been analyzing disintegrate. With willingness to change a recognized virtue, a criterion in fact of morality, differences in others will no longer be recognized as troublesome or fearful, at least openly. Nor will presumptions of superiority or inferiority attach to differences *per se*. Exclusiveness will cease to be a source of prestige. Blind efforts to produce types, to secure homogeneity, will be condemned. Suspicion of the stranger *qua* stranger will disappear. Intolerance will be a crime. The point in making everybody alike will have been lost. Variation will be welcome. There will even be a cult of variability. And to this end complete freedom of personal contacts will be sought. The play of personality upon personality will become indeed the recognized

* Professor Robinson, I find, has already put him on the defensive. "At last, perhaps, the long-disputed sin against the Holy Ghost has been found; it may be the refusal to co-operate with the vital principle of betterment. History would seem, in short, to condemn the principle of conservatism as a hopeless and wicked anachronism." (*The New History*, p. 265. New York, 1913.)

14

raison d'être of society instead of the greatest of
its apprehensions.

In this society the viability of the world will be
taken advantage of. The habit of living in lairs
will die out and with it the malady of home-
sickness. We shall live at large, truly mobilized,
going where it is best for us to be, unperturbed
by novel experience and not safeguarded against
it. Nor will our going or coming be a circumstance for apprehension or for ceremonial recognition. Hospitality as we know it will have no
part to play. There will be newcomers, but no
guests; helpers in making the newcomers feel
at home, welcomers, but no hosts. Without the
spirit of monopoly or exclusiveness, without a
fear of strangers, there is no further question of
hospitality. There will be on earth, we may say
to the Christian, as in heaven, a relation merely
between the early arrival and the late.

In this society age will not bully youth nor
youth misprize age. Seniority having no recognized rights, the older will have no justification in
being tyrannical, nor the younger in being sub-
missive. Growing up will appear to be not a
reaching out for privileges, but an attaining to
prowess and a taking on of responsibilities. Education will cease to be a process of making the young

justification of group prejudice or hostility or esteemed as motives for encroachment upon other groups. Sets of congenial persons there will be no doubt just as there are now, persons who from common interests or for endless different reasons choose to associate together as long as their interests remain the same or their reasons valid—but no longer. For them and for others there will be many meeting places for social intercourse; but little or no social machinery— no "going into society," no "round of gaieties," no "being entertained." Nor will ceremonial expression be required of feeling. In those unafraid of change, emotion will not have to be dissembled* under ceremonies or alleviated by them. Wedding and funeral, birthday and other anniversary celebration, all our ceremonial boundary marks, will be less and less called for. And with

* "But may not the undissembled show of emotion in others still be disturbing?" I may be asked, "and for reasons other than dread of change, because of envy or jealousy, because emotion in another may infringe unpleasantly in all manner of ways upon our own state of mind? After all, do not manners, in spite of their cumbersome trappings, express consideration for the state of mind of the other, a state of mind that may be quite unaffected by sex or age or position, and that he is entirely entitled to maintain?" "True," I rejoin, "and it is to personal reticence I look, to a very great enhancement of it, as a substitute in these ways for ceremonial or conventionalities. And with an enhanced reticence will go a right to privacy in all personal relationships, a right we barely conceive of to-day."

their passing too the ancient taboos upon reference to life and death will be lifted, those taboos of group, not of personal, reticence which in our modern society make only for the exploitation of emotion.   Nor will emotion be aroused, it is likely, by the mere fact of change, once change is frankly envisaged as a continuous condition.

And yet in this society, needless to say, the facts of change and of heterogeneity, age, sex, kinship, race, the characteristics arising from occupation or habitat, will not be ignored.   They will not singly or in any combination imprison anyone in a set sphere, they will not create a status; and only in so far as they affect personality will they be considered; but on this very basis it may be that in many cases they will count even more than they count now.   How those who develop old age traits will fare we have considered.   Moreover "growing old" of itself may be discouraged.   With the realisation that it cannot happen gracefully and that there is nothing superior about old age, it will have to be forgone as a cover for slackness or an excuse for selfishness.   And staying young may become more than a frivolity fit for jest.   Initiative and enterprise will be demanded of youth, enthusiasms and joy in living will be expected of it, and in it indifference or apathy will be condemned and more or less indirectly penalized. Far more will be expected of sex too, I surmise, left free to express itself, than under any repressive system. Sexual mistakes or vices will become indefensible or wholly despicable once they are clearly distinguished from crime. Love making will become part of the art of living, and inexpertness in it a subject for jest perhaps or for lament, but never a virtue to be boasted of or acclaimed. And passionate love will develop its own restraints, restraints more compelling than those imposed by kin or state or church. Such love making is incomparably more exacting than marriage in any form. More will be asked of parenthood too when based on eugenic facts than of merely juridical or proprietary parenthood. Similarly, eugenic ideas of mating may give a new and compelling significance to stock or race. Race and habitat may also play new and important parts. Everyone may be expected to live in the racial group where he is most worth while or in the climate that agrees with him and keeps him at his best. As for occupational characteristics, once the budding theory of so-called scientific management blossoms, and society loses its grotesque indifference to seeing round pegs in square holes and square in round, the fitting of the individual to his job may become imperative and obligatory. And although a man or woman may have some choice in work that is suitable, work they are unfit for they may be quite drastically forbidden.

Indeed once society becomes impatient of misfits, of waste, of futilities, it will become open to the inroads of a new kind of intolerance, terrific and appalling. Pressure upon one as an individual is capable of becoming far more severe than pressure upon one as a member of a class, and psychological standards are ever more difficult to live up to than standards of propriety. Anxious to place the individual properly according to its conception of his individuality or personality, insistent that he make the most of himself, society might in truth become a very monster of oppression.

Given a purely intellectual conception of individuality or personality and a purely rationalistic attitude towards it, such an outcome would be perhaps inevitable. But will society ever be purely intellectual or rationalistic? Will it not develop a feeling for personality mitigating its rationalism? Not merely a feeling of toleration for idiosyncrasies, a liberal attitude met quite commonly even nowadays; but a far more positive feeling, a feeling compounded of kindliness and gentleness, affectionate and yet more akin in its fearlessness to tenderness or pity than to love or rather to the love we know. That love depends on sympathy, on the sense of participation; it emphasizes the aspects we are alike in, dissembling or ignoring those in which we differ. It is love despite fear. The feeling for personality I am thinking of is a perfectly fearless love.* It is not love casting out fear, rather is it fearlessness plus love. Acknowledging to itself the existence of human differences, but unapprehensive of them, unanxious, it is a feeling distinct from the democratic spirit of fraternity or from its begetter, that love of one's fellow so appealingly given voice on the Mount by the Sea of Galilee. Fully accepting the age-old idea that men are fond of their own kind only, and to them only are good, Jew and Gentile alike overlaid their preachment of love with a fiction of homogeneity. *Egalité* was to be uttered in the same breath with *fraternité;* men were all children of the same father, all equally entitled to his consideration, equal heirs in the kingdom of heaven. This Essene representation or sentimentality was bound, like any other sentimentality, to fail.

* Are you not foreseeing in this love for personality a new "mystical, prelogical representation," I may be asked. Perhaps.

Men and women are *not* alike, nor juniors and
their seniors, nor money changers and farmers,
nor Christians and Moslems, nor English and
Germans, nor any two human beings whatsoever,
and social structures based on the dogma of their
likeness have ever been but buildings on the
sands. The wind of fear has but to blow, the
tide of distrust to rise, and great is the fall of
the dogmatists.

Neither in Christianity then nor in democracy
has the feeling which for lack of a better term I
may call a love for personality found expression.
Expression it does find, however, in life, for it is
the feeling not seldom experienced for those of
whom we have neither distrust nor fear—imper-
fectly for the very young, more integrally, in modern culture, for the dead.   In the society I foresee,
a society from which so much of our fear of one
another will have disappeared, where self-preservation in so many of its phases will be accounted a
crime against nature and not its first law, may
not the gentleness we bestow on little children
outlast their infancy and the pity which wells up
in us for the dead spend itself on the pitiful among
the living?   On the shy child and on all those
beset by the miseries of shyness; on those who
never grow up or feeling their age are old before

they need be; on those who heedless of the
treasures of passion have settled down to a passion-
less routine in marriage or in celibacy; on men
apprehensive of women or women apprehensive
of men; on men and women of position or of
property or of cultivation, and of nothing else;
on all who pride themselves on birth or nationality
or race, on belonging to a given calling or party
or organization—all victims of the hydra-headed
obsession of group consciousness; on all prisoners
of the past, bound fast by their own habits or
the habits of others; on all who in defence of
habit become the proprietors of others only to
live in constant dread of loss; on all who, seeking
mere companionship, shun the joys and sorrows
of intimacy; on all who stay poor, too fearful of
others to be enriched by them, too bewildered by
others to dare be themselves; and finally on all
sentimentalists, those timid beings who conscious
of change and yet resistant to it are for ever
dodging the facts of life and shirking its business—
on them and on those they drag with them behind
their vain defences, the empty moats and the falling walls of conventionality.

REFERENCES

PREFACE

1 EMERSON, R. W. *Manners*
2 CHESTERFIELD. *Letter* vi

I

1 JAMES, WILLIAM. *The Principles of Pyschology*, ii., 433. New York, 1902
2 *Lî Kî*, Bk. 1, sect. ii, pt. iii, 51. *Sacred Books of the East*, xxvii, xxviii
3 *Letter* iii
4 FURNIVALL, F. J. *The Babees Book*, p. 26. London, 1868. *Stans Puer ad Mensam*. About 1460 A.D.
5 ROUTLEDGE, W. S. and K. *With a Prehistoric People*, p. 3. London, 1910
6 MAYNE, ETHEL COLBURN. *Byron*, i, 72. New York, 1912
7 JAMES, ii, 433
8 DUBOIS, J. A. *Hindu Manners, Customs and Ceremonies*, p. 79. Oxford, 1899
9 FRAZER, JAMES G. *The Golden Bough: Taboo and the Perils of the Soul*, pp. 115–16. London, 1911
10 VIRCHOW, R. *The Veddás of Ceylon*, pp. 7–8. Colombo, 1888
11 SELIGMANN, p. 122
12 FRAZER, p. 103
13 *Ib.*, p. 108
14 CORYAT, THOMAS. *Coryat's Crudities*, i, 155. Glasgow, 1905
15 WILSON, C. T. and FELKIN, R. W. *Uganda and the Egyptian Soudan*, i, 210. London, 1882

II

1 WILSON and FELKIN, ii, 65

2 BINNING, i, 298
3 GARNETT, LUCY M. J. *The Women of Turkey and their Folk-Lore: The Jewish and Moslem Women*, pp. 287–8. London, 1893
4 FRAZER, p. 112
5 WILSON and FELKIN, i, 127
6 CORYAT, i, 132
7 BURCKHARDT, J. L. *Notes on the Bedouins and Wahábys*, p. 51. London, 1830
8 BATCHELOR, JOHN. *The Ainu and their Folk-Lore*, pp. 387–8. London, 1901
9 CRAWLEY, pp. 146–7
10 GOULDSBURY, C. and SHEANE, H. *The Great Plateau of Northern Rhodesia*, pp. 256–7. London, 1911
11 ROSCOE, J. "Further Notes on the Manners and Customs of the Baganda." *Journal Anthropological Institute*, xxxii (1902), 69
12 HOWITT, A. W. *The Native Tribes of South-East Australia*, p. 713. London and New York, 1904
13 BATCHELOR, p. 270
14 CRAWLEY, p. 146
15 ZEYNEB HANOUM. *A Turkish Woman's European Impressions*, p. 87. Philadelphia, 1913
16 FISON, LORIMER. *Tales from Old Fiji*, p. 163. London, 1904
17 GARNETT, pp. 33, 35
18 *Ib.*, p. 135
19 GROOT, J. J. M. DE. *The Religious System of China*, i, 25, 78–80; ii, 717. London, 1902–10; ASTLEY, TH. *A New General Collection of Voyages and Travels*, iv, 210. London, 1747
20 CORYAT, i, 394
21 SELIGMANN, C. G. *The Melanesians of British New Guinea*, p. 611. Cambridge, 1910
22 *Lî Kî*, Bk. II, sect. i, pt. i, 18
23 GARNETT, pp. 31, 33

III

1 CASTIGLIONE, BALDASSARE. *The Book of the Courtier*, p. 55. London, 1900
2 WILSON and FELKIN, ii, 15

3 *The Ainu and their Folk-Lore*, p. 156
4 *A Turkish Woman's European Impressions*, p. 33
5 *A Father's Legacy to his Daughters*, p. 101. Annexed to CHESTERFIELD, *Principles of Politeness*. Portsmouth, N. H., 1786
6 *Lî Kî*, Bk. I, sect. i, pt. iii, 7
7 HALL, FLORENCE HOWE. *Social Customs*, p. 347. Boston, 1911
8 *Lî Kî*, Bk. I, sect. i, pt. iii, 51
9 MORGAN, LEWIS H. *League of the Iroquois*, i, 319. New York, 1901
10 FURNIVALL, p. 23. Written about 1500
11 COLQUHOUN, A. R. *Among the Shans*, p. 163. New York, 1885
12 FARRAR, pp. 343–4
13 *Ib.*, p. 394
14 HALE, MRS. SARAH J. *Manners, Happy Homes, and Good Society all the Year Round*, p. 223. Boston, 1889
15 SELIGMANN, *The Melanesians*, p. 466
16 MORTON, p. 125
17 HALL, p. 336; *The Complete Hostess*, p. 284
18 *Ib.*, pp. 276–7
19 SMYTH, R. BROUGH. *The Aborigines of Victoria*, i, 133. Melbourne and London, 1878
20 SPENCER, BALDWIN and GILLEN, F. J. *The Northern Tribes of Central Australia*, p. 570. London and New York, 1904
21 ROSCOE, p. 70
22 SELIGMANN, *The Veddas*, p. 44
23 BATCHELOR, p. 192
24 *Lî Kî*, Bk. I, sect. i, pt. ii, 24
25 *Ib.*, Bk. XV, 1
26 *Ib.*, Bk. I, sect. i, pt. ii, 25
27 *Ib.*, Bk. I, sect. i, pt. ii, 28–30
28 SCHOOLCRAFT, H. R. *Indian Tribes*, pt. ii, p. 132. Philadelphia
29 *Lî Kî*, xxviii, 78 n. 2
30 HUNTER, W. W. *The Annals of Rural Bengal*, p. 216. London, 1868
31 *Journals of Expedition of Discovery into Central Australia*, ii, 304. London, 1845

32 *The Young Lady's Friend*, p. 395
33 ROSCOE, p. 53
34 *Lî Kî*, Bk. i, sect. i, pt. iii, 18–19
35 SMYTH, i, 135
36 LEARNED, MRS. FRANK. *The Etiquette of New York To-day*, p. 226. New York, 1906
37 *The Complete Hostess*, p. 282
38 *Manners and Social Usages*, pp. 14, 16
39 *The Complete Hostess*, pp. 282–3
40 *Ib.*, p. 283
41 LEARNED, p. 225
42 FARRAR, p. 399
43 BUCHANAN, JAMES. *North American Indians*, i, 23–4. New York, 1824

IV

1 KENNAN, GEORGE. "An Island in the Sea of History," *The National Geographic Magazine*, Oct., 1913, p. 1129
2 WESTERMARCK, EDWARD. *The Origin and Development of the Moral Ideas*, i, 584. London, 1908
3 WILSON and FELKIN, i, 162
4 WESTERMARCK, i, 575
5 PENNELL, T. L. *Among the Wild Tribes of the Afghan Frontier*, pp. 24–5. Philadelphia, 1909
6 MARCO POLO, i, 189–90. Edited by Yule. London, 1871
7 CRAWLEY, p. 153
8 *Ib.*
9 LIVINGSTONE, DAVID. *Travels and Researches in South Africa*, p. 96. Philadelphia.
10 BATCHELOR, p. 200
11 BINNING, i, 319
12 BURCKHARDT, p. 23
13 *Ib.*, p. 102
14 WESTERMARCK, i, 590–1
15 GOULDSBURY and SHEANE, p. 257
16 *Ib.*
17 WILSON and FELKIN, ii, 17
18 FURNIVALL, p. 102. HUGH RHODES. *The Boke of Nurture*. London, 1577
19 *Laws*, iii, 106. *Sacred Books of the East*, xxv

References 223

20 GOULDSBURY and SHEANE, p. 257
21 ROSCOE, p. 70
22 HOLLIS, A. C. *The Masai*, p. 287. Oxford, 1905
23 MAN, E. H. "On the Aboriginal Inhabitants of the Andaman Islands." *Journal of the Anthropological Institute*, xii (1882–3), 148–9
24 HALL, p. 3.7
25 BINNING, i, 323
26 GOULDSBURY and SHEANE, p. 17
27 MAN, p. 125
28 FARRAR, p. 400
29 DENNETT, R. E. *Seven Years Among the Fjort*, p. 56. London, 1887
30 *Dame Curtsey's Book of Etiquette*, p. 109
31 LEARNED, p. 227

V

1 ROUTLEDGE, p. 24
2 SMYTH, i, 135
3 CRAWLEY, p. 146; Cp. CATLIN, GEO. *North American Indians*, i, 56. London, 1866
4 BATCHELOR, p. 193
5 DUFFEY, p. 23
6 *Ib.*, p. 26
7 CASTIGLIONE, p. 142. Cp. *Reports of the Cambridge Anthropological Expedition to Torres Straits*, v, 281. Cambridge, 1904
8 HOWITT, p. 235
9 SELIGMANN, *The Melanesians*, p. 9
10 HALL, p. 278
11 *Ib.*, p. 277
12 *Ib.*, p. 278
13 *Ib.*, pp. 280–1
14 *Ib.*, pp. 279–80
15 *Ib.*, p. 288
16 SMYTH, i, 134
17 FRAZER, pp. 104–5
18 WILSON and FELKIN, i, 67
19 FRAZER, p. 103

VI

1 FRAZER, pp. 115, 125
2 *Ib.*, p. 118
3 GOULDSBURY and SHEANE, p. 27
4 FRAZER, p. 119
5 *Ib.*, pp. 120–1
6 WILSON and FELKIN, ii, 8
7 ROSCOE, p. 43
8 FURNIVALL, p. lxiii
9 CASTIGLIONE, pp. 115, 371
10 CRAWLEY, pp. 151, 160
11 FURNIVALL, p. 189
12 CRAWLEY, p. 160
13 DUBOIS, pp. 52 n. 1, 53, 61–2
14 *Letter* i
15 FRAZER, pp. 132, 135
16 *Letter* xxiii
17 SCHOUTEN, GAUTIER. *Voyage aux Indes Orientales*, i, 296. Rouen, 1725
18 DENNETT, R. E. *At the Back of the Black Man's Mind*, p. 37. London and New York, 1906
19 MARSDEN, WM. *The History of Sumatra*, p. 275. London, 1783
20 FRAZER, p. 119
21 WILSON and FELKIN, ii, 23
22 EASTMAN, C. A. *Indian Boyhood*, p. 149. New York, 1902
23 WILSON and FELKIN, i, 212
24 SAUNDERSON, H. S. "Notes on Corea and its People." *Journal Anthropological Institute*, xxiv (1894–5), 302
25 SPENCER, H., ii, 193
26 COXE, MARGARET. *Woman*, i, 236
27 WILSON and FELKIN, i, 180
28 DUBOIS, p. 20
29 SPENCER, H., ii, 206
30 FURNIVALL, p. xlvii n. 1
31 *Ib.*, p. 15. *Urbanitas*
32 WILSON and FELKIN, i, 149
33 SAUNDERSON, p. 307
34 FURNIVALL, p. xlvi

35 *Ib.*, pp. xlvii–xlviii
36 GOULDSBURY and SHEANE, p. 50
37 WILLIAMS, TH. *Fiji and the Fijians*, i, 37. London, 1858
38 HALL, p. 251
39 WILLIAMS, i, 37
40 BROWN, GEORGE. *Melanesians and Polynesians*, pp. 330–1. London, 1910. Cp. SKEAT, W. W. *Malay Magic*, p. 35. London, 1900
41 SPENCER, H., ii, 155
42 *Ib.*, ii, 153
43 DOBRIZHOFFER, M. *An Account of the Abipones*, ii, 204–5. London, 1822
44 *Letter* ii

VII

1 *Letter* i
2 FURNIVALL, p. 96. *The Boke of Nurture*, or *School of Good Maners*, ll. 509–12

VIII

1 LEARNED, p. 94
2 DUFFEY, pp. 23, 24
3 BROWN, p. 381
4 BURCKHARDT, p. 210
5 *Ib.*, ii, 125
6 II *Kings*, iv, 26
7 II *Samuel*, xviii, 28
8 DOBRIZHOFFER, ii, 137
9 MALLERY, GARRICK. "Customs of Courtesy." *The American Anthropologist*, iii (1890), 208
10 WILLIAMS, i, 152
11 BROWN, p. 381
12 SPENCER, H., ii, 133
13 BROWN, p. 378
14 *Ib.*, p. 409; WILLIAMS, i, 152
15 SPENCER, H., ii, 16
16 *Ib.*, ii, 19
17 BATCHELOR, p. 190
18 CODRINGTON, R. H. *The Melanesians*, p. 354. Oxford, 1891

19 ROUTLEDGE, p. 24
20 SPENCER, H., ii, 151
21 ROSCOE, p. 69
22 BATCHELOR, p. 190
23 COLE, H. "Notes on the Wagogo of German East Africa."
   Journal Anthropological Institute, xxxii (1902), 322
24 ROUTLEDGE, p. 24
25 WILSON and FELKIN, i, 162
26 HARVEY, GEORGE. *Women, etc.*, p. 123. New York and
   London, 1908
27 DOBRIZHOFFER, ii, 137–8
28 WILLIAMS, i, 152
29 PLOSS, H. *Das Kind*, i, 70. Leipzig, 1884
30 SELIGMANN, *The Veddas*, p. 120
31 ROSCOE, p. 29

IX

1 TERENCE, *Phormio*, Act I
2 RIVERS, p. 503
3 DANKS, B. "Marriage Customs of the New Britain Group."
   Journal Anthropological Institute, xviii (1889), 287
4 McCLINTOCK, WALTER. *The Old North Trail*, p. 187. London, 1910
5 MAN, *J. A. I.*, xi, 287–8

X

1 *Manners and Social Usages*, p. 8
2 WARD, p. 81
3 *Ib.*, p. 68
4 *Manners and Social Usages*, p. 10
5 *Ib.*, p. 26
6 WARD, p. 55
7 MORTON, p. 33
8 HALL, p. 55
9 *Ib.*, pp. 53, 55
10 WARD, pp. 57, 62, 79, 82
11 HALL, p. 53
12 WARD, p. 57; *Manners and Social Usages*, p. 2
13 WARD, p. 57
14 *Ib.*, pp. 58, 59

15 WARD, p. 56
16 *Ib.*, pp. 66–7
17 HALL, *The Correct Thing*, p. 170
18 *Ib.*, p. 178
19 WARD, p. 56
20 *Ib.*, p. 54

XI

1 *A Mission to Gelele, King of Dahome*, i, 140–3. London, 1893
2 *Ib.*, ii, 34
3 DOBRIZHOFFER, ii, 276
4 ELLIS, A. B. *The Tshi-Speaking Peoples of the Gold Coast of West Africa*, pp. 226–7. London, 1887
5 PARSONS, *The Old-Fashioned Woman*, pp. 25–6
6 URLIN, ETHEL L. *Dancing, Ancient and Modern*, p. 103· New York, 1913
7 *A Mission to Gelele*, ii, 9
8 ZEYNEB HANOUM, p. 33
9 DENNETT, *At the Back of the Black Man's Mind*, p. 209
10 BATCHELOR, p. 270
11 ROUTLEDGE, p. 111
12 FRIČ, V. and RADIN, P. "Contributions to the Study of the Bororo Indians." *Journal Anthropological Institute*, xxxvi (1906), 388
13 PARKER, K. L. *The Euahlayi Tribe*, p. 132. London, 1905
14 *With a Prehistoric People*, p. 202
15 *Lî Kî*, xxviii, 80 n. 2
16 Pp. 238–9
17 WARD, p. 158
18 *Ib.*, p. 157
19 *Ib.*
20 *Ib.*, p. 160
21 FARRAR, p. 342
22 *Ib.*, p. 343
23 WARD, p. 160
24 CRAWLEY, 173

XII

1 SELIGMANN, *The Veddas*, p. 68
2 Bk. I, sect. i, pt. iii, 31

228   References

3 GRIFFIS, W. E.   *Corea*, p. 245.   New York, 1907
4 GARNETT, p. 233
5 *An Account of the Abipones*, ii, 139
6 FURNIVALL, p. 46
7 BURCKHARDT, p. 23
8 GRIFFIS, pp. 244, 250
9 HOLMES, J.   "Initiation Ceremonies of Natives of the
     Papuan Gulf." *Journal Anthropological Institute*, xxxii
     (1902), 425
10 CODRINGTON, R. H.   *The Melanesians*, p. 87.   Oxford,
     1891
11 COLQUHOUN, *Amongst the Shans*, p. 51
12 HODSON, T. C.   *The Nāga Tribes of Manipur*, pp. 45-6, 77.
     London, 1911
13 ROUTLEDGE, p. 121
14 ROSCOE, p. 53
15 *The Second Part of Youths' Behavior* or *Decency in Conversa-
     tion Amongst Women*, p. 156.   London, 1664
16 *Crudities*, i, 368
17 CASTIGLIONE, p. 220
18 *Ib.*, p. 89
19 SPENCER, BALDWIN and GILLEN, F. J.   *The Native Tribes of
     Central Australia*, p. 509.   London and New York, 1899
20 SELIGMANN, *The Melanesians*, pp. 459 n. 1, 466
21 FURNIVALL, p. 15
22 Bk. i, sect. 1, pt. iii, 33
23 *Ib.*, Bk. 1, sect. i, pt. iii, 36
24 MAN, XII, 355
25 MORTON, p. 206
26 HOLLIS, pp. 286-7
27 WESTERMARCK, EDWARD.   *The History of Human Marriage*,
     p. 373.   London and New York, 1901
28 BURCKHARDT, p. 37
29 WESTERMARCK, *Marriage*, pp. 370-73
30 *Ib.*, pp. 363-4, 366, 368
31 FRAZER, pp. 103-4
32 *Pygmies and Papuans*, p. 206
33 SELIGMANN, *The Veddas*, p. 44
34 PARKER, E. H., p. 97
35 BURCKHARDT, p. 200

36 STEINMETZ, S. R. *Ethnologische Studien zur ersten Entwicklung der Strafe*, ii, 351. Leiden und Leipzig, 1894
37 FURNESS, W. H. *The Home-Life of Borneo Head-Hunters*, p. 169. ' Philadelphia, 1902
38 PARSONS, ELSIE CLEWS (JOHN MAIN). *Religious Chastity*, ch. xv. New York, 1913
39 CASTIGLIONE, p. 48
40 PARSONS, *Religious Chastity*, p. 278
41 *Science and Health*, pp. 61–2. Boston, 1904
42 CRAWLEY, p. 219
43 HOWITT, p. 402
44 CRAWLEY, p. 188
45 LIVINGSTONE, p. 97
46 EASTMAN, p. 106
47 *The Self-Tormentor*, Act IV
48 TERENCE, *The Mother-in-Law*, Act II
49 CRAWLEY, p. 221
50 ROSCOE, pp. 70, 77
51 BATCHELOR, p. 255

XIII

1 *The Mother-in-Law*, Act I
2 Act II
3 DANKS, pp. 286–7
4 LEWIN, T. H. *Wild Races of South-Eastern India*, pp. 202–3. London, 1870
5 GARNETT, p. 257
6 PARSONS, ELSIE CLEWS. *The Family*, p. 141. New York and London, 1906
7 WESTERMARCK, *Marriage*, p. 450
8 ASTLEY, ii, 240
9 WESTERMARCK, *Marriage*, p. 450
10 SMITH, W. ROBERTSON. *Kinship and Marriage in Early Arabia*, p. 133. Cambridge, 1885
11 SAUNDERSON, p. 303
12 GRIFFIS, p. 247
13 CRAWLEY, p. 394
14 HOLLIS, pp. 286–7
15 *Religious Chastity*, chaps. iii, viii
16 *The Principles of Psychology*, ii, 394–5

230   References

17 DONALDSON, JAMES. *Woman*, p. 61. London, New York,
     Bombay, and Calcutta, 1907
18 MAYNE, ii, 164–5
19 WILLIAMS, i, 152
20 BATCHELOR
21 GARNETT, p. 237
22 *Journals*, ii, 214–5
23 MAN, xii, 94 n. 2
24 *Journal Anthropological Institute*, xxix (1899–1900), 339
25 LUBBOCK, JOHN. *The Origin of Civilization*, p. 51. London,
     1870
26 CRAWLEY, p. 180
27 SELIGMANN, *The Melanesians*, p. 506 n. 1
28 *American Anthropologist*, New Ser. iii (1901), 617

                              XIV

1   DANKS, pp. 283–4
2   WESTERMARCK, *Marriage*, p. 303
3   *Ib.*, pp. 298, 305
4   HOWITT, p. 185
5   WESTERMARCK, *Marriage*, p. 367
6   CRAWLEY, p. 400
7   GOULDSBURY and SHEANE, p. 259
8   CRAWLEY, p. 400
9   STARCKE, C. N. *The Primitive Family*, p. 238. New York,
     1889
10 FRAZER, *Totemism and Exogamy*, i, 541
11 CRAWLEY, pp. 402–3
12 WILLIAMS, i, 136
13 Bk. i, sect. i, pt. iii, 32
14 GOULDSBURY and SHEANE, p. 259
15 GARNETT, LUCY M. J. *The Women of Turkey: The Christian
     Women*, p. 203. London, 1890
16 HOWITT, A. W. "The Jeraeil, or Initiation Ceremonies of
     the Kurnai Tribe." *Journal Anthropological Institute*, xiv
     (1884–5), 306; *Native Tribes*, p. 402
17 HOLMES, pp. 421, 422
18 WEBSTER, p. 24
19 CRAWLEY, p. 216
20 *Personal Communication*

21 FRAZER, *Totemism and Exogamy*, i, 542

22 CRAWLEY, p. 217

23 SELIGMANN, *The Veddas*, p. 69

24 STARCKE, p. 239 n. 4. But cp. SELIGMANN, *The Veddas*, p. 69

25 CRAWLEY, p. 218

26 JENKS, A. E. *The Bontoc Igorot*, pp. 50–1, 62. *Ethnological Survey Publications.* Manila, 1905

27 FRIČ and RADIN, p. 388

28 HAGEN, B. *Unter den Papua's*, p. 234. Wiesbaden, 1899

29 FURNIVALL, p. xiv

30 *Ib.*, p. lxii

31 ELLIS, W. *Polynesian Researches*, i, 263. London, 1853

32 BURCKHARDT, pp. 201–2

33 JOHNSTON, H. *The Uganda Protectorate*, ii, 735. New York and London, 1902.

34 CRAWLEY, 152

35 *Reports of the Cambridge Anthropological Society to Torres Straits*, vi, 281. Cambridge, 1908

36 PARSONS, *The Old-Fashioned Woman*, pp. 177–8

37 HOWITT, *Native Tribes*, p. 748

38 MAN, xii, 126

39 GRIFFIS, p. 261

40 SELIGMANN, *The Melanesians*, pp. 484–5

41 McCLINTOCK, p. 187

42 WESTERMARCK, *Marriage*, p. 317

43 DORSEY, J. OWEN. "Teton Folk-Lore." *The American Anthropologist*, ii (1889), 157

44 ROTH, WALTER E. *Ethnological Studies among the North-West Central Queensland Aborigines*, p. 134. Brisbane and London, 1897

45 MAN, E. H. "On Andamanese and Nicobarese Objects." *Journal Anthropological Institute*, xi (1881–2), 288

46 RIVERS, pp. 33–4

47 GOULDSBURY and SHEANE, p. 257

48 *Lt Kî*, Bk. x, sect. i, 7

49 *The Second Part of Youths' Behavior*, p. 17

50 *The Young Lady's Friend*, p. 203

51 *R. C. A. E. T. S.*, v. 148

52 *Lt Kî*, Bk. x, sect. i, 4

232   **References**

53   FARRAR, p. 222
54   *Wild Races of South-Eastern India*, p. 181

XV

1   LÉVY-BRUHL, pp. 410–11
2   GRIFFIS, p. 246
3   SELIGMANN, *The Melanesians*, p. 60
4   PARKER, E. H., p. 94
5   ROUTLEDGE, pp. 25, 141
6   HOWITT, *Native Tribes*, p. 769.
7   WEBSTER, p. 67
8   HODSON, p. 183
9   WEBSTER, p. 69
10   SELIGMANN, *The Melanesians*, pp. 139, 454
11   ROUTLEDGE, p. 202
12   Bk. III, sect. v, 3
13   EASTMAN, p. 52
14   COLE, p. 317
15   WEBSTER, p. 70
16   *Ib.*, p. 87
17   EASTMAN, p. 59
18   *Personal Observation*
19   ROUTLEDGE, p. 24
20   HALL, G. STANLEY.   *Adolescence*, ii, 252.   New York, 1905
21   WEBSTER, p. 40
22   PLOSS, ii, 447–8
23   WEBSTER, p. 54
24   BURCKHARDT, p. 28
25   ASTLEY, iv, 77
26   *Autobiography of an Elderly Woman*, p. 69.   Boston and New York, 1911
27   CORYAT, i, 399
28   *Lî Kî*, Bk. III, sect. v, 5
29   *Ib.*, Bk. I, sect. i, pt. ii, 18
30   CASTIGLIONE, p. 107
31   ROUTLEDGE, pp. 137–8
32   *Ib.*, p. 140
33   *Ib.*
34   *R. C. A. E. T. S.*, vi, 115

References 233

35 MacDONALD, J. "East Central African Customs." *Journal Anthropological Institute*, xxii (1892–3), 101
36 DONALDSON, p. 144
37 CASTIGLIONE, p. 119
38 FRAZER, *Totemism and Exogamy*, i, 477
39 WEBSTER, p. 90
40 ROUTLEDGE, p. 143
41 *Indian Boyhood*, p. 67
42 COLE, p. 325
43 MacDONALD, DUFF. *Africana*, i, 63–4. London, Edinburgh, Aberdeen, 1882
44 *R. C. A. E. T. S.*, vi, 140
45 *Essays for Young Ladies*, pp. 174–5. London, 1777
46 WEBSTER, pp. 92, 93
47 *Ib.*, p. 90
48 FRAZER, *Totemism and Exogamy*, i, 542
49 WEBSTER, p. 90
50 *Lî Kî*, Bk. I, sect. i, pt. ii, 1; pt. iii, 3
51 EASTMAN, p. 58
52 *Letter* lii
53 *Autobiography of an Elderly Woman*, pp. 193–4
54 SMYTH, i, 137
55 ROUTLEDGE, p. 23
56 HOLLIS, pp. 285–6
57 FARRAR, p. 211
58 *R. C. A. E. T. S.*, v, 214
59 WESTERMARCK, *Moral Ideas*, i, 604
60 *Lî Kî*, Bk. I, sect. i, pt. ii, 21
61 FURNIVALL, p. 16. Written about 1480
62 *Lî Kî*, Bk. I, sect. i, pt. iii, 60
63 GOULDSBURY and SHEANE, p. 259
64 GRIFFIS, p. 259
65 *Native Tribes*, p. 22
66 *Laws*, ix, 16
67 HILTON–SIMPSON, M. W. *Land and Peoples of the Kasai*, p. 92. Chicago, 1912
68 SELIGMANN, *The Melanesians*, p. 70
69 WEBSTER, pp. 27–8
70 *Ib.*, p. 81
71 CRAWLEY, p. 160

72 WEBSTER, p. 89
73 MAN, xii, 344
74 FARRAR, p. 348
75 HOLLIS, pp. 287–8
76 SELIGMANN, *The Melanesians*, pp. 460, 470–1
77 *The Self-Tormentor*, Act III
78 WEBSTER, pp. 88–9
79 ROUTLEDGE, p. 187
80 *A Turkish Woman's European Impressions*, p. 156

XVI

1 RIVERS, p. 370
2 PARSONS, *Religious Chastity*, pp. 65–9
3 MARTYR, PETER. *The Decades of the New World or West India*, First Decade, Bk. IX, sec. 46, in *The First Three English Books on America*. Westminster, 1895

INDEX

Abipones, 70, 82, 87, 110, 120
Address, 49 n., 68, 69–70, 166
 –7; 178–9; titles of, 69 n.,
 143
Aenezes. *See* Arabs
Afghans, 35
Africa, Central, 6; East, 165,
 184; South, 187, 193; West
 Coast of, 57, 63, 71, 83, 151,
 168, 199 n.
Age-classes, vii, viii, ix, x, 29
 n., 47, 48, 50, 76, 77, 82, 99,
 100–1, 116–7, 123, 124, 163
 ff., 176 ff., 205, 207, 208,
 210–11
Ainu, 10, 12, 13, 20, 26, 36,
 38 n., 45, 83, 85, 112, 131,
 132, 150, 182 n.
Akikúyu, 3, 44, 84, 86, 112,
 122, 178, 180, 181, 183, 185,
 190, 196
Albania, 9–10, 120, 140, 145 n.,
 150
Aleuts, 128, 142
Andamanese, 40, 41, 95, 124,
 144, 150, 166, 171, 194
Arabs, 10, 37, 48, 81, 84, 121,
 125, 127, 141–2, 165, 182
Armenians, 160
Ashantee, 59
Avoidance, x, 1 ff., 94, 95, 131,
 158 ff., 211
Awemba, 11, 37, 39, 41, 56, 68,
 84, 86, 111, 158, 160, 192

Baduwis, 4, 55
Baganda, 3, 7, 12, 26, 28, 34,
 38, 39, 57, 64, 65, 88, 122,
 132. *See* Mutesa
Balonda, 83
Banks' Islands, 83

Baralongs, 126
Basuto, 160
Bechuana, 193
Beni-Amer, 158
Benin, 54, 111–12
Betrothal, 88, 89, 91, 93, 96,
 138, 166, 171, 178
Birth, 88, 89, 93, 171, 193
Birthdays, 91, 170, 212
Blackfeet, 94–5, 168
Blackfellows, 5, 11, 12, 13,
 25, 28–9, 36, 45, 50, 54, 112,
 123, 129, 142, 150, 157, 158,
 159, 161, 162, 166, 171, 177,
 179, 181, 185, 187–8, 190,
 192, 193, 198 n.
Borneo, 3 n., 127, 144
Bororo, 112, 163
Bowing, 68–9, 83, 109
Burma, 83
Bushmans, 126
Bushongo, 192
Byron, 4, 139 n., 148–9

Calling. *See* Visiting
Caribs, 142
Caste, viii, ix, x, 2, 8 n., 29, 38,
 55 ff., 101, 115–6, 123, 125–6,
 205, 206 n., 211, 218
Cazembe, 56, 60
Celibacy, 47, 145–6, 177, 186,
 218
Chesterfield, Lord, viii, 3, 8, 19,
 60, 61, 70, 74–5, 189
Chinese, 2, 6, 15, 16, 18, 21, 22,
 26–7, 28, 35–6, 49 n., 53 n.,
 55, 84, 90, 102 n., 112, 119–
 20, 123, 125, 157, 159, 172,
 173, 180, 182, 183, 189, 191
Chivalry, 73 ff., 131
Chukmas, 174

235

Index